# FOUNDATIONS OF HISTORY

# The American West

**MARJORIE GODFREY**

Heinemann

Heinemann Library
Halley Court, Jordan Hill, Oxford OX2 8EJ
a division of Reed Educational and Professional
Publishing Ltd

MELBOURNE AUCKLAND FLORENCE PRAGUE MADRID
ATHENS SINGAPORE KUALA LUMPUR TOKYO
SAO PAULO CHICAGO PORTSMOUTH NH (USA)
MEXICO CITY IBADAN GABORONE JOHANNESBURG
KAMPALA NAIROBI

© Marjorie Godfrey 1996
The moral rights of the proprietor have been asserted

All rights reserved. No part of this publication may be reproduced, stored in a retrieval system, or transmitted in any form or by any means, electronic, mechanical, photocopying, recording, or otherwise without either the prior written permission of the publishers or a licence permitting restricted copying in the United Kingdom issued by the copyright Licensing Agency Ltd, 90 Tottenham Court Road, London W1P 9HE.

First Published 1996
Paperback Edition Published 1997

00 99 98 97 96
10 9 8 7 6 5 4 3 2 1

British Library Cataloguing in Publication Data is available from the British Library on request.

ISBN 0 431 05831 8      (0431 058261  PB) (973.8)

Produced by Visual Image, Street, Somerset
Illustrated by Visual Image, Jane Watkins
Printed by Mateu Cromo in Spain
Cover design by The Wooden Ark Studio
Cover photo: *Pehriska-Ruhpa Hidatsa Man* by Karl Bodmer. Reproduced by permission of the Joslyn Art Museum, Omaha, Nebraska; gift of the Enron Art Foundation.

**Acknowledgements**
The publishers would like to thank the following for permission to reproduce photographs:

American Heritage Center, University of Wyoming: 74 below, 77 below, 80 centre below; Arizona Historical Society, Tucson: 74 top left; Art Resource, New York/National Museum of American Art, Washington: 17; Baker Library, Harvard Business School: 64; Bancroft Library, University of California, Berkeley: 34; Buffalo Bill Historical Center, Cody, Wyoming: 21/ Gift of Mrs J Maxwell Moran 11/ Werner Forman Archive: 23/ Gift of Barbara S Leggett: 54; / Gertrude Vanderbilt Whitney Trust Fund purchase: 93 top;/ Gift of William E. Weiss: 18, 20; Butler Institute of American Art, Youngstown, Ohio: 31; Colorado Historical Society: 87; Denver Public Library, Western History Department: 8, 45, 60; Mary Evans Picture Library: 36, 39; Gilcrease Museum, Tulsa, Oklahoma: 46, 50, 58; Joslyn Art Museum, Omaha: 19; Kansas State Historical Society, Topeka: 29, 44, 52 below, 67, 74 top right; Mansell Collection: 26, 38; Montana Historical Society, Helena: 76; Nebraska State Historical Society: 66; Peter Newark's Western Americana: 5, 24, 33, 47, 52 top, center, 53, 55, 56, 59, 61, 71, 73, 78, 80 top, 83, 89, 91, 93 below; Oxford Scientific Films/ Roland Mayr: 16; South Dakota State Historical Society, Pierre, South Dakota: 10; Warner Bros (courtesy John Kobel Collection): 4; Western History Collections, University of Oklahoma Library: 70, 77 top left, right, 79.

The publishers have made every effort to trace copyright holders of material in this book. Any omissions will be rectified in subsequent printings if notice is given to the publisher.

**Written sources**: In some sources the wording has been simplified to ensure that the source is accessible.

E.C. Abbott, *We Pointed them North*, University of Oklahoma Press 1966: 5.3C

Ralf K. Andrist, (quoted in) *The Long Death*, Macmillan Company (New York) 1964: 8.1A, 8.2A - M

J.I.H. Baur (ed.), *Autobiography of Worthington Whittredge*, Brooklyn Museum Journal, 1842: 1.2B

S.M. Barret (ed.), *Geronimo, his own Story*, Abacus, Sphere Books, 1974: 2.3F

Dee Brown, *Bury My Heart at Wounded Knee*, Holt, Rinehart and Winston, 1971: 8.3A

George Catlin, *Manners, Customs and Condition of the North American Indians, Vol 1*, Dover Publications Inc, New York, 1844: 2.1B, 2.3D, 2.3G, 2.4A, 2.4D; Vol II, 2.5A

William Clayton, *A Daily Record of the Journey of The Original company of Mormon Pioneers from Nauvoo to the Valley of the Great Salt Lake*, Salt Lake City, 1921: 3.3F

Henry Commager, (ed.) (quoted in) *The West*, Orbis Publishing Co, 1976: Page 29, 3.2A, B, C, D, 4.1F, 6.1, B, C, D, 6.3B, D

*Early Western Travel Series*, Vol xvii, Arthur H. Clark and Company, 1904: 1.2A

J. Evetts Haley, *Charles Goodnight: Cowman and Plainsman*, University of Oklahoma Press, 1949: 5.3F, 5.3H

Odie B. Faulk, *The Crimson Desert*, OUP, 1974: 2.5C

J.G. Fraser, *The Native Races of America*, Lund Humphries, 1939: 2.4B

W. Grasswasking, *Proceedings of Denver County Court*, Frink, Jackson and Spring, University of Colorado Press, 1956: 5.2D

E.A. Hoebel, *The Cheyenne*, Holt, Rinehart and Winston, 1978: 2.5B

Royal B. Hassrick, *The American West*, Octopus Books Ltd, 1975: 5.3E

Luther Standing Bear, *My People the Sioux*, University of Nebraska Press, 1975: 2.1A, 2.4E

Robin May, (quoted in) *History of the American West*, Hamlyn, 1984: 4.1C, 5.3E

Robin May, (quoted in) *The Story of the Wild West*, Hamlyn, 1978: 7.1B, 7.1C, D, G, H

Joseph McCoy, *Historic Sketches of the Cattle Trade of the West and South West*, Kansas City, Missouri: 5.3I

Clyde A. Milner, Carol A. O'Connor, Martha A. Sandweiss (eds.) *The Oxford History of the American West*, OUP, 1994: 1.3A, 1.4A, 1.4B, 5.1A

W. Mulder and A.R. Mortensen, *Amongst the Mormons*, Alfred A. Knopf, 1958: 3.3B

J. Neihardt (ed.), *Black Elk Speaks*. Spere Books, 1974: 2.2D

Francis Parkman, *The Oregon Trail*, 1847: 2.3C

Schools Council History 13-16 Project, (quoted in) *The American West 1840-95,* Holmes, McDougall, 1977: 3.1F, G, 5.2E, 5.3H, 7.1E, 7.1G

Jennifer and Martin Tucker, *The American West*, Basil Blackwell, 1986: Page 69

O.D. Winter, (ed.) *A Friend of the Mormons, Thomas L Kane*, San Francisco, California, 1937: 3.1E

Derek Wise, *The American West*, Macmillan, 1984: Page 32

This book is for the pupils and staff at Hodgson High School.

# CONTENTS

**CHAPTER 1   FANTASY, FACTS AND FRONTIERS**
- 1.1   America - the beginning .................................. 4
- 1.2   America - the land .......................................... 6
- 1.3   Who went West? ............................................. 8
- 1.4   What did the West have to offer? ................... 10
- 1.5   How did the USA govern itself? ..................... 12
- 1.6   Why was there an American Civil War? ........... 13

**CHAPTER 2   THE WORLD OF THE PLAINS INDIANS**
- 2.1   Who were the Plains Indians? ......................... 15
- 2.2   The struggle for survival ................................. 16
- 2.3   Everyday life in the Indian villages ................. 20
- 2.4   What were the beliefs of the Plains Indians? ... 23
- 2.5   How did the Indians govern themselves? ......... 26
- 2.6   How do we know about Indian culture? ........... 28

**CHAPTER 3   TRAILBLAZERS**
- 3.1   The first trailblazers? ...................................... 29
- 3.2   All that glisters - is it gold? ............................ 32
- 3.3   The Mormons: migrants of another sort ......... 36
- 3.4   The Mormons after Brigham Young ................. 43

**CHAPTER 4   TRAINS TO CROSS A CONTINENT**
- 4.1   What transport preceded the railways? ........... 44
- 4.2   How was the railway built across the USA? ..... 47
- 4.3   What impact did the railways have? ............... 48

**CHAPTER 5   CATTLEMEN AND COWBOYS**
- 5.1   How did the cattle industry begin? ................. 50
- 5.2   Who was behind the 'beef bonanza'? .............. 51
- 5.3   Who were the cowboys? ................................. 54
- 5.4   Why did the cattle trade rise and fall? ............ 59
- 5.5   From high plains to Hollywood ....................... 61

**CHAPTER 6   HOMESTEADERS ON THE PLAINS**
- 6.1   What made the homesteaders go West? ......... 62
- 6.2   What was life like on the Plains? .................... 66
- 6.3   A tough life for women ................................... 67
- 6.4   How did the homesteaders adapt to the Plains? ... 68
- 6.5   What was the 'Sooner State'? ......................... 71
- 6.6   The American Dream ...................................... 71

**CHAPTER 7   HOW WILD WAS THE WEST?**
- 7.1   Why was the West hard to police? ................. 72
- 7.2   The Johnson County War ................................ 79
- 7.3   The end of the 'wild' West .............................. 81
- 7.4   The Lincoln County War 1877–81 .................... 81

**CHAPTER 8   HOW THE PLAINS WERE WON AND LOST**
- 8.1   Why did the Indians go on the warpath? ........ 82
- 8.2   The Indians' struggle for freedom ................... 84
- 8.3   Conflicting attitudes to the Indian problem .... 90
- 8.4   From the Little Bighorn to Wounded Knee ...... 91
- 8.5   Evaluating General Custer .............................. 95

**INDEX** .................................................................. 96

# CHAPTER 1

# FANTASY, FACTS AND FRONTIERS

*The stranger rides into town. No one knows who he is but he looks like trouble. Rumours fly as he heads for the saloon. The good-time girls eye him with interest. The gamblers fall silent at their tables. The stranger downs his drink and slowly turns. Another drinker rises to face him. 'This town,' he spits, 'ain't big enough for the both of us.' They go for their guns . . .*

▶ A scene from the film *Wyatt Earp*, 1994.

'Western' books and films have been popular for years: cowboys and Indians, gunslingers and cattle rustlers. Many of these stories have been made up but some of their characters really did live. You might have heard of Billy the Kid, Sitting Bull, Butch Cassidy and Jesse James. They were all real people, living in an important and exciting period of history in the USA.

Between 1840 and 1895 a huge area of the USA, which we call the American West, was taken over by white people. The Indians already living there were eventually pushed out.

This first chapter will describe the main groups of people who were involved. But first, you need to know about the history and geography of the USA.

## 1.1 America – the beginning

### The Indians
In 1492 Christopher Columbus tried to find a new route to India. He sailed west from Europe. Instead of reaching India he landed on the coast of America. When he met the native people of America he called them Indians. The name has remained.

### The White settlers
Over the next 200 years people sailed from Europe and settled along the east coast of America. This land became part of the British Empire. In 1783, at the end of the War of Independence with Britain the settlers formed their own country, the United States of America.

▲ The growth of the United States of America 1783–1853.

## What was the 'American West'?

To the west of the first thirteen states were the Appalachian Mountains. These made the boundary or **frontier** of the USA in 1783. Then, the West was all the land over the mountains. As settlers moved the frontier changed. The West always was the land to the west of the frontier. In 1840, when the frontier was the Mississippi River, the West meant the land to the west of that river.

The map above shows how during the 1800s the US Government came to own all the land from the Atlantic Ocean to the Pacific Ocean.

▶ This is Sitting Bull, a famous chief of the Sioux tribe who tried to stop the US government confining the Plains Indians to reservations in the 1860s and 1870s. He and another Sioux Chief, Crazy Horse, fought against General Custer at the Battle of the Little Bighorn in 1876 (see Chapter 8).

# 1.2 America – the land

The map on page 7 shows the physical features of the USA as it is today.

The earliest European settlers lived along the east coast of America. They had the sea at one side and the Appalachian Mountains on the other side. Those settlers who did cross the mountains found that there was fertile farmland in the valley of the Mississippi River. They could farm successfully on this land.

## The Great American Desert

Some travellers went further and explored the land beyond the Mississippi. They found a huge area of grassland now known as the Great Plains. There were some rivers but in most areas water was scarce. There were few trees so building homes would be difficult. There was always a strong wind. This wind dried the land in summer and brought blizzards and freezing cold in winter.

So the travellers decided that this land would not be suitable for farming. School books written in the 19th century called this area the Great American Desert (see Sources A and B).

## The Rocky Mountains and Plateaux region

After crossing the Great American Desert travellers would have to climb the Rocky Mountains. They might have met hunters and trappers who were looking for bears, beavers and mountain lions. Travellers would then go down to another barren and windswept area called the Plateaux region. In this area is the Great Salt Lake which is important in our story.

## The Sierra Nevada and the Pacific coastlands

Once more travellers would have to cross mountains, this time the Sierra Nevada. Some of the snow-capped peaks are 4,500 metres high. This was the final hurdle.

Beyond these mountains there was good farming land along the west coast of the USA. The soil was fertile and the climate was warm. The states of California and Oregon are in this area.

### Source A

The Great Plains are almost wholly unfit for cultivation [to farm], and of course uninhabitable by a people depending upon agriculture for their living . . . the scarcity of wood and water will make it difficult to settle here.

▲ A description of the Great Plains by Major Stephen Long, 1819–20.

### Source B

Whoever crossed the Plains with its herds of buffalo and flocks of antelope, its wild horses, deer and fleet rabbits, could hardly fail to be impressed with its vastness and silence.

▲ From the *Autobiography of Worthington Whitteredge*, published in the *Brooklyn Museum Journal*, 1842.

### A DESERT LAND

The Indians of the Great Plains did not see them as a desert. They saw them as home. The land and everything on it was a gift from their God.

| | |
|---|---|
| Eastern lowlands. | The Rocky Mountains. Heavily wooded in the South, home to grizzly bears and beavers. |
| Low Plains (long prairie grass) — The Great Plains – called the Great American Desert because of the winds and extremes of hot and cold. | **The Plateaux Region** – Columbia Plateau, semi-desert. The Great Basin – very dry, includes the Great Salt Lake. Colorado River Plateau – canyons and deep ravines. Sierra Nevada – high, forested mountain range forming a barrier between the Plains and the Pacific coast ands. |
| High Plains (short grass) | |
| | Pacific coastlands – *California* and *Oregon*. Warm and fertile. |

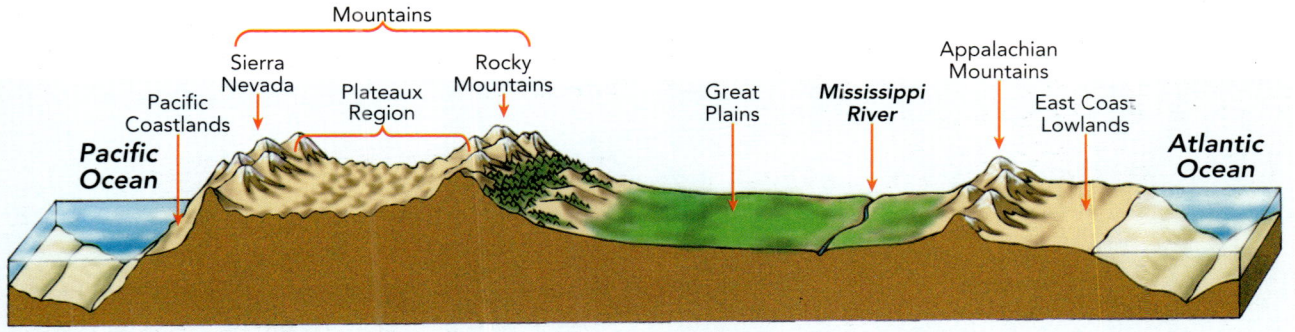

▲ The geographical regions of the United States.

1.2 AMERICA – THE LAND

# 1.3 Who went West?

The story of the West is about people on the move. Some settlers moved West and some returned home. Some followed later to join friends and family. Some, especially the Indians, were forced to move as their land was 'invaded'.

## Who were the first American pioneers?
A pioneer is someone who blazes or opens up a trail where others might one day follow. The first pioneers of the West were farmers and gold miners.

## The farmers
Trappers and mountain men, who roamed the mountains hunting animals for their fur, told stories about good fertile land far away over the mountains. So the farmers who could not find land in the east struggled in their covered wagons right across America to Oregon and California. They travelled across the Plains and over the mountains, attracted by the promise of good land where crops would grow.

### Source A
In 1800 there were 450,000 settlers farming land west of the Appalachian Mountains. In 1850 there were 1,500,000.

▲ These figures are taken from the official US Census results for 1800 and 1850.

## Settlers in Oregon and California
By 1845 there were about 6,000 settlers living in Oregon. California was more difficult to reach because less was known about the trails that led there. Then something happened to make California very popular.

## The Gold Rush
Gold was found in 1848 and by 1849 90,000 prospectors rushed to California. Mining camps and then towns were built.

### Source B

◀ A Mormon family, pictured with handcarts on the trail in northern Utah in 1867 (see page 42).

8 CHAPTER 1 FANTASY, FACTS AND FRONTIERS

## More settlers

### 1 The Mormons

The **Mormons** were also pioneers. They were badly treated because of their religious ideas and way of life. To escape this they went westwards in 1847. They finally settled near the Great Salt Lake. The land here was very poor but they still managed to grow crops. The Mormons built Salt Lake City and later founded the state of Utah.

▲ The first settlers in the West in the late 1840s and the 1850s.

### 2 Homesteaders

Between 1854 and 1865 the first homesteaders (farmers) began to settle on the Great Plains, in Kansas and Nebraska. Many came from the eastern states. But some of them were former Negro slaves who had been freed in 1865. Later more and more of the homesteaders were immigrants from Europe searching for a better life. Life was difficult for the first homesteaders on the Great Plains. But it became easier when the railway was completed in 1869.

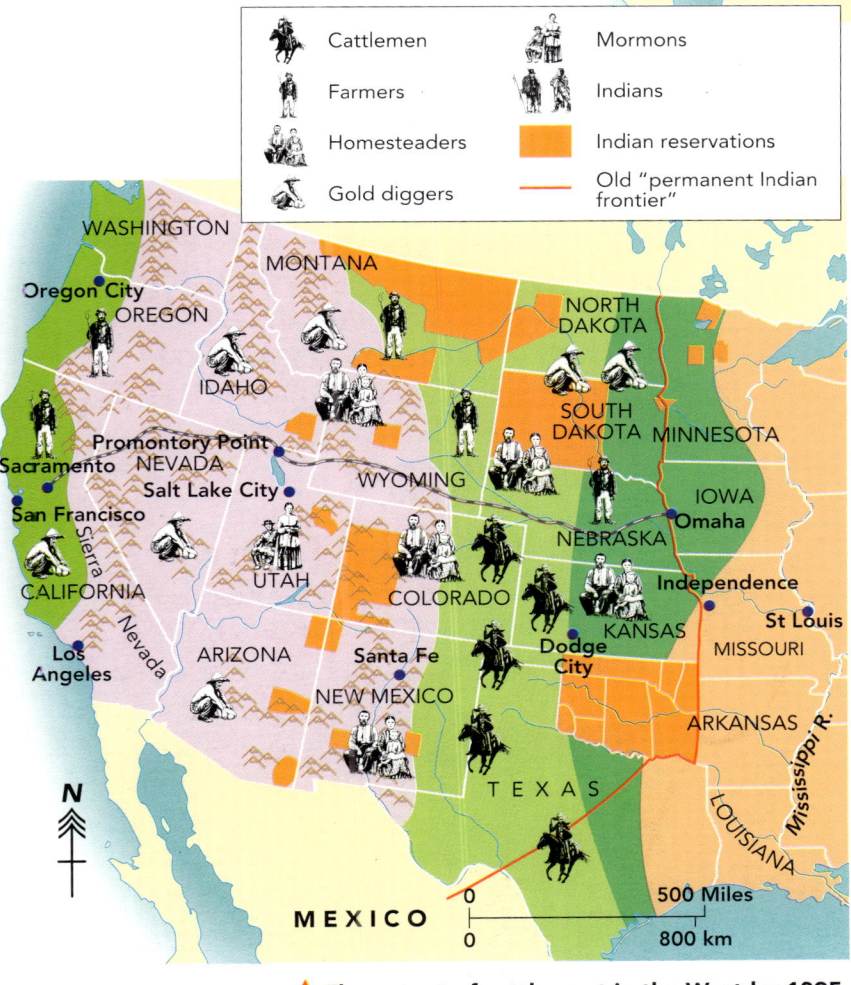

▲ The extent of settlement in the West by 1895.

## 3 Cattlemen

Each summer from 1866, cattlemen from Texas drove herds of Texas Longhorns northwards across the Plains to meet the railway. Cow towns such as Dodge City, Abilene and Sedalia grew up along the railway. From these towns, cattle were taken to the cities of the East or the mining towns of the West. The cattle business boomed from the 1860s to the mid 1880s.

## Problems between the cattlemen and the homesteaders

Gradually, cattlemen began to set up ranches on the Plains. But there were no fences and the cattle were allowed to graze freely on the open range. Often they roamed on to the homesteaders' land and destroyed the crops. This caused arguments between the homesteaders and cattlemen.

# 1.4 What did the West have to offer?

### Cheap land
Land was available in the West. Some of it was cheap; some of it was even free. This encouraged settlers to go because land in the East was very expensive.

### A land of opportunity
Newspaper articles and letters described how good life was in the West. This convinced farmers, businessmen, teachers, churchmen, lawyers and would-be politicians to move West. There were jobs for all these people in the new, growing settlements.

### Religious freedom
Many people, like the Mormons, went West so they could worship as they wanted.

## Source A

▲ A poster published by South Dakota to attract settlers.

## Source B

Up to and including 1880 the country had a frontier [boundary] of settlement, but at present there can hardly be said to be a frontier line.

▲ Extract from the official census report of 1890.

## Who encouraged people to go West?

### 1 Governments of new territories
When settlers moved to a new area it was called a **territory** at first. It could not become a **state** until there were 60,000 people living there. So the governments of the new territories set out to attract more settlers. Once it became a state, a territory was able to govern itself without much interference from the US government.

### 2 The US Government
The US Government also wanted settlers to move to the West. It made sure that land was not expensive. It passed laws such as the **Homestead Act**, which allowed land to be sold at very low prices. This encouraged people to migrate West. The Government also published maps to help travellers find their way and sent army units to protect them.

> **Source C**
>
> ... our manifest destiny is to overspread the continent allotted by Providence for the development of our yearly multiplying millions.
>
> ▲ John L. O'Sullivan, editor of the *Democratic Revue*, July 1845.

## What was manifest destiny?
This was the belief that the white Americans should settle and govern all the land from the Atlantic to the Pacific. It was something the white Americans believed they had to do.

**Source D**

▲ A painting by William Ranney called *Advice on the Prairie* (1853). In the early 1850s, when mass migration on to the Plains had just begun, settlers travelled in family groups in covered wagons.

Most white Americans, especially the politicians at the nation's capital, Washington, believed strongly in manifest destiny. This was why the US Government obtained land in America from other countries. It is also another reason why the Government took land from the Indians and encouraged white settlers to move West.

# 1.5 How did the USA govern itself?

## The need for unity
After the War of Independence, the British stopped ruling America. The thirteen states had to find a way to rule themselves and become a nation. They had to trade with other countries, and be able to defend themselves. They had to find ways to organize and govern the land beyond the Appalachian Mountains where new settlers were starting to go. So in 1787 they created a **constitution** (a set of rules) to guide the new country.

## The needs of individual states
Although the thirteen states knew they had to work together on some things, there were other things each state wanted to decide. So the constitution stated that some decisions were made by the US Government for all the states, but other things could be decided by the individual states.

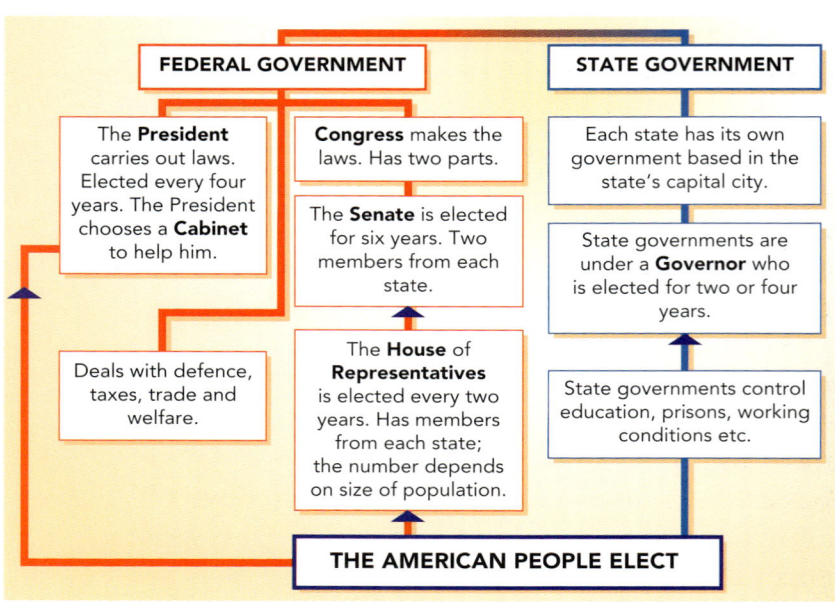

▲ The system of government in the USA.

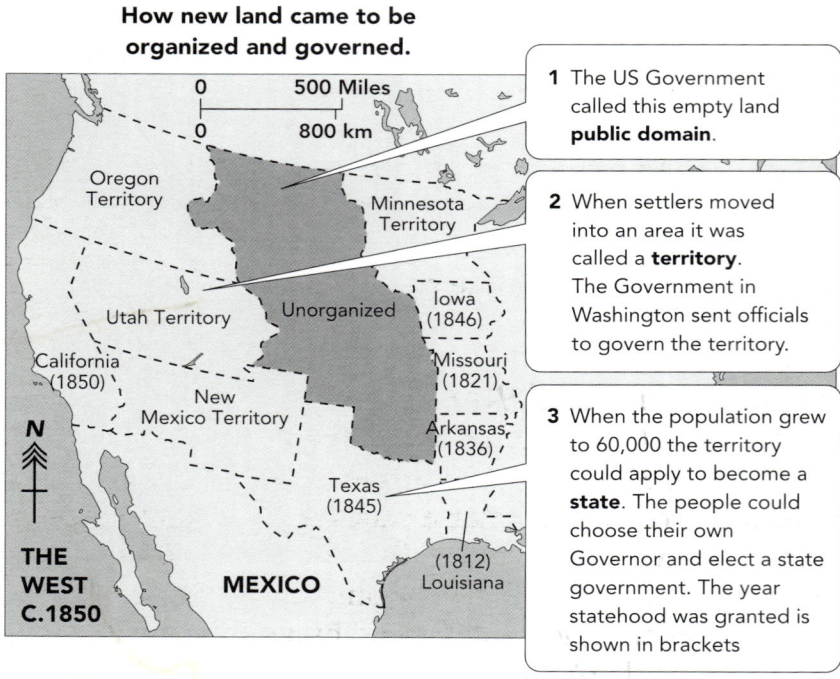

## Federal Government
The US has a **federal** system of government. This means that there is a central government in Washington that makes important decisions on things that affect all the states, like defence.

## State Government
Each state also has a government of its own that meets in the state capital. The state government passes laws about things like education and law and order.

# 1.6 Why was there an American Civil War?

The thirteen states did not get on well. They disagreed on **slavery**. The southern states had many cotton and tobacco plantations, where the work was done by slaves. The northern states were mainly made up of farmers and merchants who did not agree with slavery.

## What did the Constitution say?

The Constitution protected the freedom of the individual. Did this mean there should be no slaves? The Constitution promised to protect property. The plantation owners in the South said that their slaves were valuable property. As settlers moved West a decision had to be made. Was slavery to be allowed in the new territories?

## The American Civil War

In 1860 South Carolina decided to break away from the USA. Other southern states followed. The northern states wanted to keep the states together. In 1861 the American Civil War began. The problem was whether states could break away from the USA and have their own form of government.

In 1865 the Civil War ended in victory for the northern states. Individual states could not now break away from the USA. Slavery was **abolished**.

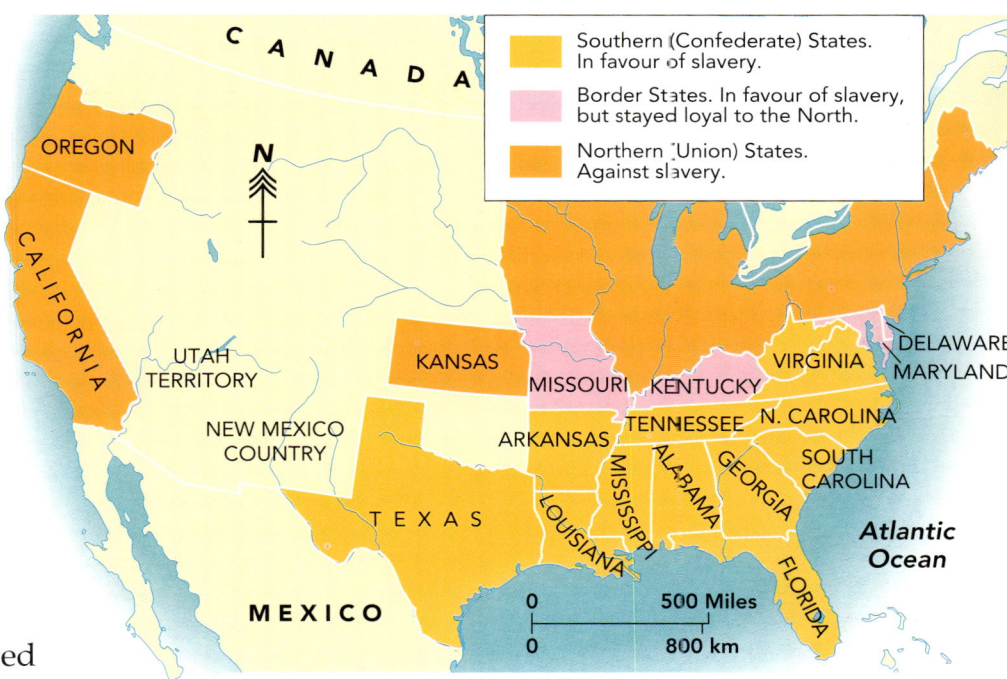

▲ The divisions between the Northern and Southern states in the Civil War 1861–5.

# SUMMARY

▶ **1840** The Mississippi River was the western frontier of the USA.

▶ **1843** The first settlers arrived in Oregon.

▶ **1846–7** The Mormons travelled to the Great Salt Lake.

▶ **1848–9** Gold rush began in California.

▶ **1850s** The first homesteaders began to move on to the Plains.

▶ **1861–5** Civil War between northern and southern states.

▶ **1865** Slavery abolished.

▶ **1866** The first 'long drive' of Texas Longhorns across the Plains.

▶ **1869** A railway was completed across America.

▶ **1870s** Cattle ranching began on the Plains.

# CHAPTER 2

# THE WORLD OF THE PLAINS INDIANS

The huge area of land that lies in the middle of North America is called the Great Plains. The pioneers of the 1840s called it the Great American Desert. They crossed it as quickly as possible because they did not want to live there. They wanted to reach the fertile lands of Oregon and California where they could farm.

The Great Plains, which seemed barren and hostile to the pioneers, was the home of the Plains Indians. There were many different Indian tribes living on the Great Plains (see map). Most tribes hunted the buffalo herds. They were nomads (wanderers) following the buffalo herds around the Plains.

This chapter describes the world of the Plains Indians, which was very different from that of the white settlers. When the white settlers started moving on to the Plains it made some kind of clash between the two groups very likely.

## Source A

We did not think of the great open plains, the beautiful rolling hills, and winding streams with tangled growth, as 'wild' . . . To us it was tame.

▲ Luther Standing Bear, *My People the Sioux*, 1975.

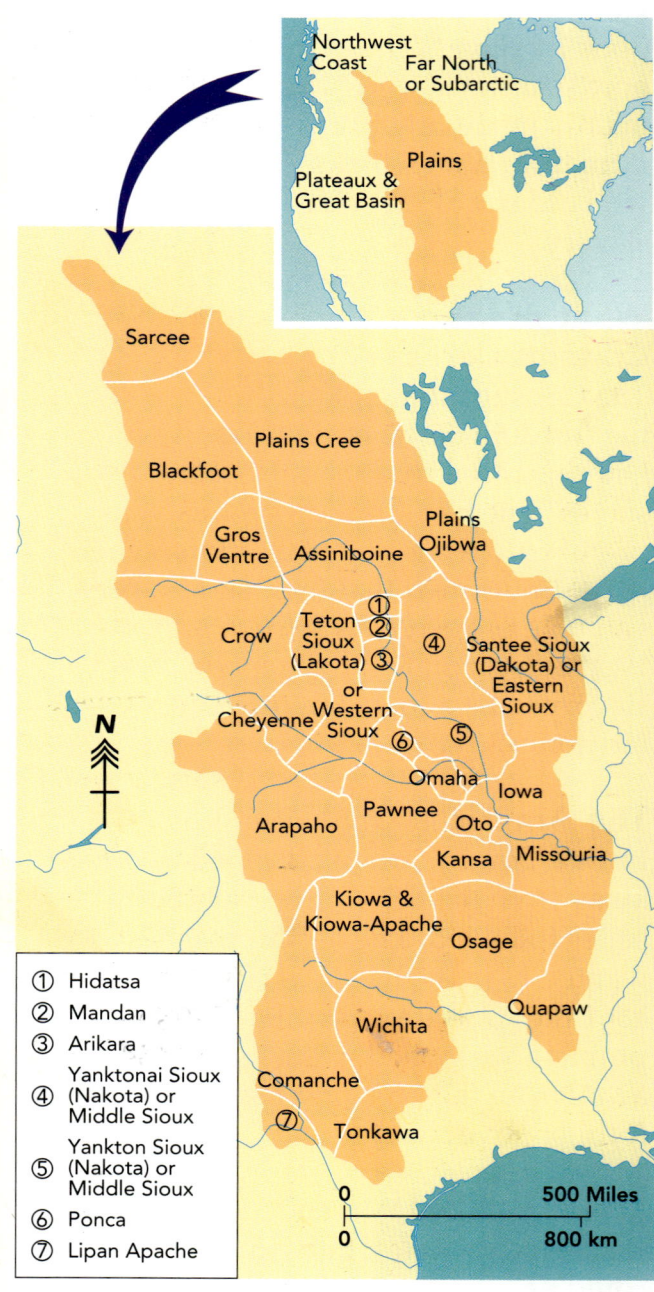

▲ The area occupied by the Plains Indians and where the different tribes were based in the 19th century.

14 CHAPTER 2 THE WORLD OF THE PLAINS INDIANS

# 2.1 Who were the Plains Indians?

## Differences between tribes

There were more than 30 different Indian tribes living on the Great Plains. Each tribe had its own language. The history of each tribe was not written down but stories were handed down by the older Indians to the younger ones.

Each tribe had its own special decorations on their moccasins (soft leather shoes), parfleches (large rawhide bags), saddles and tipis (tent-like homes).

Each tribe had its own area of land on the Plains. For example, the Blackfoot tribes lived in the northern Plains, the Sioux and Cheyenne in the central Plains and the Comanche on the southern Plains.

## Similarities between tribes

Almost all the tribes on the Plains hunted the buffalo. They needed to do this to get food to survive. Huge herds of buffalo roamed the Plains so the Indians had to be on the move to follow the buffalo and hunt them. The Indians had a **nomadic** way of life and lived in tipis which could easily be moved.

Some tribes, like the Mandans, who lived on the edge of the Plains, grew some crops. Because the Mandans were not always on the move, they built shelters rather than living in tipis (see Source A on page 17).

▲ A Blackfoot Indian.

▶ A Dakota Sioux.

▲ Assiniboine with horned headdress.

# 2.2 The struggle for survival

## Why was the buffalo so important?

At first many Indian tribes grew crops as well as hunting the buffalo. By the 19th century most of them had given up farming. Instead they came to rely completely on the buffalo. When Indians killed a buffalo they used almost every part of the animal (see diagram).

The buffalo roamed in huge herds. This meant that the Indians had to travel about the Plains to find the herds, so they lived in tipis. This nomadic way of life also influenced the Indians' family life, their ideas about bravery and their laws. If the buffalo was destroyed so, too, would be the Indian way of life.

## Tribes and bands

The Indians did not actually stay together as a tribe. There were too many people in a tribe to do this. If the whole tribe went hunting together they would kill too many buffalo from the same herd.

The whole tribe came together only in the summer in a huge tribal gathering. The rest of the time the tribe was divided into smaller groups or **bands** made up of several families. The Indians from each band would go hunting. They would not kill more buffalo than they needed. The Indians only went hunting when their supplies of dried buffalo meat were used up. Then a buffalo herd had to be found for fresh meat.

The **hide** was used to make clothes, tipis, moccasins, parfleches (bags for carrying belongings), harnesses and shields.

**Shoulder blades** and **bones** used to make hoes, knives and sledge runners. The **skull** was decorated and used in religious rituals.

**Horns** used to make head-dresses, spoons, cups and powder-flasks. **Hooves** used to make glue and tools.

The *tongue* used to make hairbrushes and also provided food.

The **flesh** was eaten raw, or boiled, roasted or dried.

**Hair** used to stuff pillows, cushions and saddles.

**Fur** was used for blankets, saddle covers and gloves.

## How did the Indians find the buffalo?
Sometimes young braves went out to find a herd. Sometimes the tribes used the spirit world to find buffalo. They did this through dances.

George Catlin, who travelled and lived among the Plains Indians, described a buffalo dance in the Mandan tribe (see Source B).

## What did the Dog Soldiers do?
When the Indians found a herd, the village was quickly moved. This was usually organized by a special group of braves. In the Cheyenne tribe this group was called the Dog Soldiers. They protected the moving village and chose the next camp site. They made sure that the buffalo herds were not frightened away and not too many were killed. This meant the buffalo would not be wiped out.

### Source B

About ten or fifteen Mandans at a time join in the dance, each one with the skin of the buffalo's head [or mask] with horns on, placed over his head, and in his hand his favourite bow or lance, with which he is used to slay the buffalo.

This dance never fails, nor can it, for it cannot be stopped until 'buffalo come'. Drums are beating and rattles are shaken, and songs and yells are shouted, and onlookers stand ready with masks on their heads, and weapons in hand, to take the place of each one as he becomes tired.

During this time 'lookers' are kept on the hills in the neighbourhood of the village. When they discover buffaloes in sight they give the signal, by 'throwing their robes'. At this, there is a shout of thanks to the Great Spirit! These dances sometimes continue for two and three weeks without stopping.

▲ A description of a Mandan buffalo dance as seen by George Catlin in the 1830s.

### Source A

◀ Painting by George Catlin of a Mandan buffalo dance (1833). Notice the dome-shaped lodges of the Mandans.

## The buffalo hunt

For hundreds of years the Indians hunted the buffalo on foot. They had to get very close to an animal to kill it. They only had short bows and arrows so they needed to be very skilful.

In the 16th century Spanish settlers arrived in America and brought horses with them. The Indians quickly learnt to become skilful horse riders and rode in the buffalo hunt. It still took a lot of courage to get so close to a buffalo to kill it (see Source C). Young braves showed their skill and bravery in the hunt. They became respected and honoured by the rest of the tribe.

## The importance of horses

Horses were very valuable to the Indians. At first they traded for horses. Then some tribes started to breed their own. They would trade them with other tribes for guns and ammunition. Some tribes, like the Shoshoni Indians, put their most precious possessions around their horses necks. Indians would even go to war to capture horses. An Indian who had horses was a wealthy Indian.

### Source D

The crier came around the village calling out that we were going to break camp... The crier said, 'Many buffalo, I have heard! Your children, you must take care of them!' He meant to keep the children close while travelling, so that they would not scare the buffalo.

The advisers found a place to camp. Then the crier shouted, 'Your horses make ready! We shall go forth with arrows. Plenty of meat we shall make!'

Then the head man picked out the best hunters with the fastest horses, and he said, 'Young warriors, your work I know is good; so today you will feed the helpless. You shall help the old and the young and whatever you kill shall be theirs.'

This was a great honour for young men.

▲ Black Elk, holy man of the Oglala Sioux, remembers the preparation for a buffalo hunt. He was born in 1863.

### Source C

◀ *The Buffalo Hunt* painted by Frederick Remington in 1890.

## Women and the hunt

While the men were hunting, the women were busy in the new camp. They had many jobs to do.

- They prepared fires for the feast after the hunt.
- They collected branches and sticks to make frames. The buffalo meat was hung on the frames to dry.
- Later they had to clean and dry the buffalo skins. The women stretched the animal skins out with pegs to dry. Then they used scrapers, made of sharp bone, to remove any meat left on the skin.
- When the skins had dried the women made them into clothing, tipis, baby carriers called cradle boards (see below) or bags for storing food. These were beautifully decorated. The women used dyes to colour them. In some tribes they made beautiful patterns with porcupine quills and beads. This took a lot of time and skill.

Indian women who were good at decorating could join a society. For example, women in the Cheyenne tribe could join the **Quiller** society. This gave them some importance in the tribe.

### Source E

▲ A Cree woman by Karl Bodmer (1833). Her deerskin dress is a typical Plains style as are her shell and bead ear-rings. The tattoos on her chin were more common among the Cree tribe than other tribes.

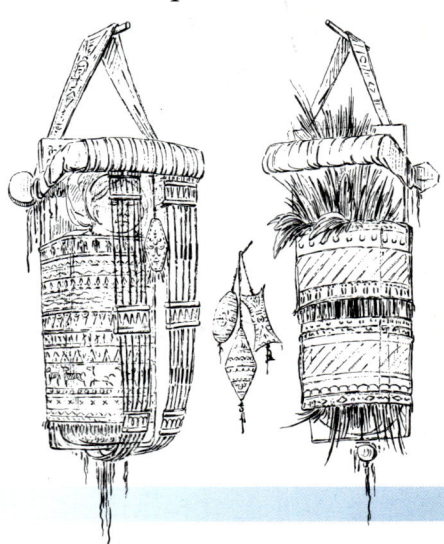

### PAINTED FACES

Not all Indians painted their faces when they went to war. Only some tribes did this. Tribes painted their faces for other reasons, for example to show happiness or sadness. Each colour had a meaning. In some tribes women painted their faces before they married. Indian braves used paint to show their tribal origins.

2.2 THE STRUGGLE FOR SURVIVAL

# 2.3 Everyday life in the Indian villages

## Tipis

Women made the tipis. Firstly, a cone-shaped framework of wooden poles was made. This shape was used because it stood up to the strong winds on the Plains.

The women sewed together buffalo hides to make a huge semi-circular cover. This was put over the wooden poles. There were flaps at the top which could be moved depending on the direction of the wind. They were to stop the smoke from the fire from going back inside. The cover was usually decorated. The Blackfeet, for example, painted colourful animals and birds on their tipis.

## What was a travois?

The women took down the tipis when it was time to move camp. This could be done very quickly and the poles, covers and family's possessions could be easily packed on a sledge or **travois** (see Source B). This was pulled by hand or harnessed to a dog or horse.

### Source A

▲ Typical Indian tipis. Usually the tipis would be more widely spaced, probably in a circle.

### Source B

◄ A painting by Charles Russell called *Indian Women Moving Camp* (1898). Using horse's helped women in their work. Notice the travois behind.

20 CHAPTER 2 THE WORLD OF THE PLAINS INDIANS

## Cradle boards

The women carried their babies in baby carriers called **cradle boards** (see page 19). Babies were encouraged not to cry because a noisy baby could cause a herd of grazing buffalo to stampede.

## The different roles of men and women

Each member of the tribe had an important role to play. The men hunted and fought. The women provided food, clothing and homes. In the Mandan tribe, women grew crops and looked for food such as wild turnips.

## Indian children

Children had to learn to be tough to survive on the Plains. They were never beaten but were punished in other ways.

### Source C

Indian parents were fond of their children, whom they never punished except in extreme cases, when they threw a bowl of cold water over them.

▲ Written by Francis Parkman in 1840. Parkman (1823–93) was an historian, traveller and writer who lived among the Indians during the 1840s.

### Source D

When we were about to leave the village, I saw a very aged and thin man, who . . . was to be left to starve. His children were preparing to be on the march. He told them to leave him.

'I am old', he said, 'and too feeble to march. My children our nation is poor, and it is necessary that you should all go to the country where you can get meat. I am a burden to my children. I cannot go and I wish to die.'

▲ George Catlin, *Manners, Customs and Condition of the North American Indians*, 1844. Catlin (1796–1872) spent a lot of time among the Indians in the 1830s.

### Source E

▶ A picture of an Indian family entitled *Days of Long Ago* painted by Henry Farny in 1903. By this time, the traditional lifestyle of the Indians had been totally destroyed.

## Source F

Being seventeen years of age, I was admitted to the council of warriors. Now I could marry Alope. She was a slender, delicate girl and we had loved each other for a long time. Her father . . . he asked many ponies for her.

In a few days I appeared before his tipi with the herd of ponies and took with me Alope. This was all the marriage ceremony necessary in our tribe.

▲ Geronimo, an Apache chief, describes his marriage.

## Source G

The son of this chief, a youth of eighteen years distinguished himself by taking four wives in one day! I visited the tipi of this young man, and saw his four little wives entering very happily on the duties of married life . . . In this country polygamy is allowed, for where there are two or three times the number of women than there are men, such an arrangement answers a good purpose, for the females are taken care of.

▲ George Catlin commenting on a polygamous marriage.

## INDIAN NAMES

In some Indian tribes children were named by their mothers. In other tribes the grandmother and the Medicine Man did this.

Most Indian names show the Indian closeness to nature – for example, 'Running Bear', 'Two Moons' and 'Black Elk'.

## Growing up

Children were prepared for their future lives by working hard. Boys were taught to ride and use their bows and arrows. They went on their first hunt at the age of fourteen.

Parents celebrated the success of their son's first hunt. They were also proud of their daughters first menstrual period because this showed she had become a woman.

## How did old people help?

Old men told stories about the history of the tribe. This helped the children to have a pride in their ancestors. When old people became helpless they were left to die. (See Source D, page 21.)

## The Indian attitude to marriage

In some tribes marriages were arranged but in most tribes a young man could choose a wife. He tried to impress her by his bravery in a buffalo hunt. Girls were told by their mothers and grandmothers never to accept the first proposal of marriage. Fathers expected the young men to offer a gift, preferably horses. When the couple became engaged they would exchange rings made of metal or horn.

There were more women than men so men could have more than one wife at a time. This is called **polygamy**. It made sure that no woman was left on her own.

## Divorce

An Indian woman owned the tipi that she had made, items such as buffalo hides and the children. A man could divorce his wife simply by saying that he would divorce her. If his wife owned the tipi he would have to return to his mother's tipi. Divorce was quite rare!

# 2.4 What were the beliefs of the Plains Indians?

## Source A

I have heard it said by some who have been preaching the Christian religion, that Indians have no religion but only ignorant superstition. I say that the North American Indian is a highly moral and religious being.

◀ George Catlin, *Manners, Customs and Condition of the North American Indians*, 1844.

## Source B

Young men pray for some animal or bird to come to them. For five or six days they neither eat nor drink, and become very thin. They dream, and whatever animal or bird they see in their dreams becomes their medicine and guardian through life.

▲ J.G. Frazer in *The Native Races of America* (1939) describing an Indian ritual.

▼ A robe decorated with the circle design which had great religious significance.

## Ideas about nature

The Plains Indians had a great respect and love for nature. They believed that they shared the land with all living things. This meant that people could not buy or sell land because it belonged to the natural world: plants, birds, animals and humans.

They believed that since all living things came from the natural world, after death, they would all return to the earth. This idea of the **cycle of life** going from birth to death led to the circle being important in Indian life.

## Nature's great circle

The Plains Indians believed that:

- Life is a circle from childhood to old age. Very old people sometimes behave like children again.
- The seasons of the year go in a circle from spring through to winter and then back into spring.

Everything around the Plains Indians seemed to be in circles. Even Indian villages and tipis were circular. So the circle was very special to the Plains Indians. It was also used to decorate tipis, clothes and other possessions.

## Source C

## A world of spirits

Almost all of the Indian tribes believed that a god, known as the Great Spirit, created the whole of nature. This explains why the Indians respected all living things. The Indians believed that the world was full of spirits. Every tree, plant and animal had its own spirit which the Indians had to have on their side. So they took part in ceremonies to call on the spirits to be with them. (See Source B on page 23.)

## What was Indian medicine?

The Indians called these spirits their 'medicine'. Young braves had to find out which animals and plants were their own special 'medicine'. A young brave had to fast (not have any food or drink), then he had to pray and wait. He would dream of an animal or bird. The creature that was in his dream would be his guardian spirit. The brave then had to find the animal, kill it, and make the skin into a 'medicine bag'. He was told what to put into the bag in his dream and the bag became a charm. He kept the bag with him and no one else could touch it.

## What did medicine men do?

Medicine men had special powers. They were wise and had many jobs. They

- cured people who were ill
- gave advice to chiefs and elders
- explained dreams.

Medicine men were also in touch with the spirits. To give them extra power to do these things they often wore the skins of an animal.

## Animal power

Indians believed that some animals were very powerful. Some tribes looked for a special toad to help them when they were hunting the buffalo. The Blackfoot tribe believed that the beaver would help them find food.

### Source D

After there had been a long drought, and all the crops dried up, the young men were ordered to start the ceremony to bring clouds and rain. They always succeeded because this ceremony went on day and night until it rained.

▲ George Catlin describing a Mandan rain-making ceremony in the 1830s.

▼ Medicine man of the Hidatsa tribe, in the costume of the Dog Dance, painted by Karl Bodmer, in about 1834.

### Source E

An old man would come forward with a very sharp pointed knife. He would take hold of the breast of the young brave, pull the skin forward and pierce it through with the knife. Then he would insert a wooden pin . . . through the slit and tie a strong buckskin thong to this pin.

From the pole two rawhide ropes were suspended. The brave would now be lifted up . . . and was hanging from his breast . . . Although the blood would be running down from the knife incision, the brave would smile, although everyone knew he must be suffering intense pain.

▲ Description of a Sun Dance from *My Family the Sioux*, by Luther Standing Bear. In the Sioux tribe, young men sometimes did this when someone in the family was ill.

## How did the Indians contact the spirits?

Sometimes all the Indians in a band wanted to get in touch with the spirits for a special reason. They did this by carrying out special dances. They would do this before going to war. Sometimes it was to celebrate victory or bring rain. It could be to ask for help in hunting the buffalo.

The Mandan sometimes did a buffalo dance when they needed to find out where the herds were located (see Source A on page 17).

The most common dance was the Sun Dance. It was performed so young braves could show their courage. They did this by hanging from ropes which were fastened to their flesh by pegs. This was very painful and the braves usually fainted after about twenty minutes. The medicine man was in charge of this 'dance'. He decided when it should end. In some tribes braves even had fingers or toes cut off.

Other tribes such as the Cree, used the Sun Dance ceremony to get in touch with the spirits by praying and not by torturing themselves. These dances were an important part of the religious life of the Indians.

### SUMMARY

- Indians believed in the great circle of nature.
- Indians believed in spirits which gave 'medicine' or charms to help them.
- Medicine men could contact spirits to help the Indians.
- The power of animals was believed to be very important
- Dances were an important part of the religion of the Indians.

### SACRIFICES

Sacrifices were an important part of Indian religious life. The Pawnees were the only tribe that seem to have sacrificed humans. In most tribes, Indians sacrificed something precious to them – for example, a dog or horse. A white buffalo's skin was a good sacrifice.

## 2.5 How did the Indians govern themselves?

In Chapter 1 you read about how white Americans governed themselves. Because the Indians were always on the move they had to have a different type of government (see diagram).

### How powerful were the chiefs?
At the tribal council the chiefs sat in a huge circle. They smoked a ceremonial pipe which they thought would help them to make the right decisions. They could not force their decisions on the tribe. They could only give advice, so a band within a tribe could do as it pleased.

### Soldier societies
In each band the chief and council of elders were usually helped by soldier societies. Every man in the band could belong to one of these if he proved himself in some way. For example, the Kiowa tribe had a society called the Kaitsenko (the ten bravest). This group always led attacks on the enemy.

The Cheyenne tribe had six soldier societies. One of these – the Dog Soldiers – you read about on page 17.

▲ The Chief of the Mandan tribe.

### Source A
The chief has no control over his subjects, nor any other power except that of **influence**. [This] he gains by his virtues and his deeds in war.
He is no more than a **leader** whom every young warrior may follow, or . . . go back from . . . if he is willing to meet the disgrace that awaits a brave who deserts his chief.

▲ George Catlin describing the government of the Indians.

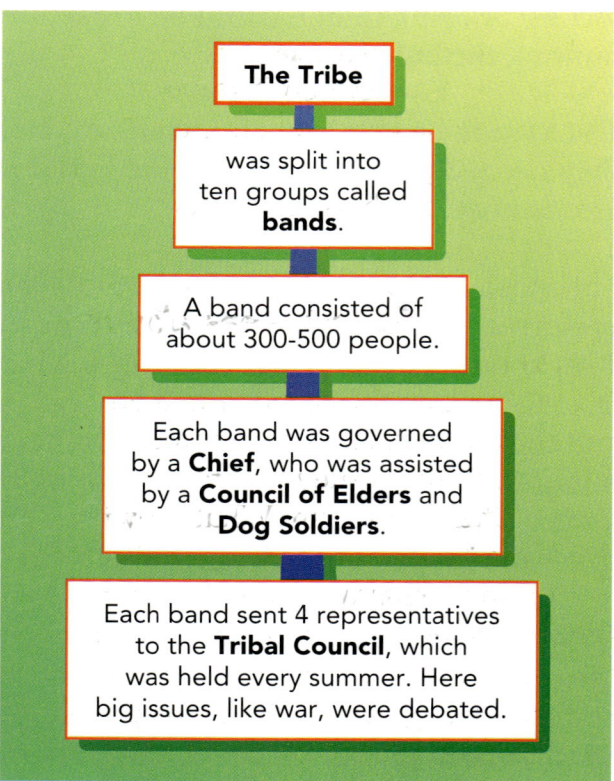

**The Tribe** was split into ten groups called **bands**.

A band consisted of about 300-500 people.

Each band was governed by a **Chief**, who was assisted by a **Council of Elders** and **Dog Soldiers**.

Each band sent 4 representatives to the **Tribal Council**, which was held every summer. Here big issues, like war, were debated.

▲ How the Cheyenne tribe was governed.

26 CHAPTER 2 THE WORLD OF THE PLAINS INDIANS

## Indian punishments

Indians did not have laws in the way we have. A nomadic tribe which was always on the move, could not have law courts and prisons so punishments were different from ours. Indians were expected to behave in a certain way. If an Indian in the Cheyenne tribe murdered someone he was expelled from the band. In some tribes the murderer was forced to look after the family of his victim. To steal a horse from an enemy was not a crime to the Indians.

## War between tribes

Many of the tribes on the Plains, such as the Comanches and the Apaches, were traditional enemies. They fought each other

- to get more horses,
- and to protect their hunting grounds.

We have seen that Indians lived in bands and each band could go its own way. Wars made the bands in the tribe join together to fight the enemy. A band was not strong enough to survive entirely on its own.

## Two very different ideas about bravery

Indians fought with bows and arrows, tomahawks and, later, with guns. They killed an enemy if they had to, but that was not their main aim. What they tried to do was to touch the enemy with a special stick. This was called a **coup stick**. This meant that the brave had to get very close to touch his enemy. He had to have courage and skill. The number of enemies he touched was counted up. This was called **counting the coup**.

### Source B

War has been changed into a great game in which scoring against the enemy is more important than killing him. The scoring is in the counting of coup – touching or striking an enemy with hand or weapons . . . A man's rank as a warrior depends on two things: his 'score' in coups, and his ability to lead raids in which Cheyenne losses are low. Killing and scalping do not rate as highly as the show-off deeds.

▲ From a book about the Cheyenne written in 1978.

### Source C

The Indian idea of bravery was different from that of the European settlers. The Comanche thought it stupid to fight when there was no chance of winning anything apart from honour; instead they would slink away, to return another day to steal horses, and take captives.

▲ Odie B. Faulk *The Crimson Desert*.

The number was recorded by cutting a feather in a certain way. This feather was then worn as a kind of symbol of achievement.

This was not understood by the white people. Using a coup stick and 'creeping up' on enemies was seen as cowardice, not bravery. White people believed in facing the enemy. To be killed in battle was an honour.

White people thought that Indians saw war as a game. Certainly Indians had no intention of being killed. A dead Indian could not get food for his family or his band. So to die was not a sign of bravery to the Indian. If he thought he was going to be killed, then he retreated.

### Why did Indians scalp their enemies?

Scalping was the cutting off of the skin and hair which covered the skull. The main reason for an Indian taking a scalp was that by doing this he believed he was taking his enemy's spirit. The enemy could not then go to the afterlife. When the Indian got to the afterlife his enemy would not be there. Sometimes an Indian survived being scalped but still believed he had lost his spirit.

### Differences grow

So the white settlers and the Indians had very different values and attitudes. Many white settlers thought the Indians were 'savage' and 'uncivilized'. Indians could not understand white people who wanted to own land, dig it up for gold and destroy the buffalo. From 1840 as more white settlers moved west into the Plains, the Indian way of life was threatened.

## 2.6 How do we know about Indian culture?

We can find out about the Indian way of life by looking at paintings and photos taken at the time. We can study things the Indians made that have been preserved (clothing, buffalo skins, cradles, even medicine bags and gambling games). We can also read written accounts.

### George Catlin (1796–1872)

Catlin travelled among the Plains Indians in 1832. He wrote about and painted pictures of life among the Indian tribes he stayed with. These included the Lakota, Blackfoot, Crow and Mandan Indians.

Catlin painted and drew over 600 pictures of Indians on his travels, which he called his 'Indian Gallery'. It is a clear and careful record of the most important aspects of everyday life in the tribes he stayed with.

### Karl Bodmer (1809–93)

Bodmer was born in Switzerland. He studied as a draftsman, so was trained to produced careful and accurate drawings. He travelled to America in 1833–4 with Prince Maximilian of Wied-Neuweid. He was hired to illustrate the book the Prince intended to write about the expedition.

Bodmer and the Prince met Mandan and Blackfoot Indians and travelled in the Rocky Mountains. Bodmer painted individual Indians, tribal activities (like buffalo hunts) and views. *Travels in the Interior of North America* was published in 1844. There were two books of writings and a book of 81 of Bodmer's paintings.

### Black Elk (born 1863)

Black Elk was an Oglala Sioux. He was born in 1863 and lived through the Battle of the Little Bighorn (where Custer was defeated by the Indians) in 1876. Black Elk went on to become Medicine Man for his tribe. He lived through the massacre of Wounded Knee in 1890. His book, *Black Elk Speaks*, provides a vivid picture of the lifestyle of the Plains Indians.

# CHAPTER 3
# TRAILBLAZERS

'It is on the stroke of seven; the rushing to and fro, the cracking of whips, the loud command to oxen... The clear notes of the trumpet sound in the front; the pilot and his guards mount their horses, the lead wagons move out of the encampment and take up the line of march, the rest fall into their places with the precision of clockwork...' And so began a typical day on the great trek West across America described by Jesse Applegate in 1843.

This chapter is about the people who blazed the first trails (routes) over the Mississippi River into the unknown; the mountain men, the animal trappers, the farmers, the gold-diggers and the Mormons. Some were greedy, some were desperate. They all were brave. Thousands were to follow in their wagon tracks.

## Jim Bridger: profile of a mountain man

Bridger was born in 1804 in Virginia. He became a fur trapper in 1822. In 1824 he went on a beaver-hunting expedition, and discovered the Great Salt Lake. In 1830 he built Fort Bridger on the Oregon Trail, a stopping place for travellers. The fort had a workshop and a forge.

During the 1850s Bridger bought a farm. He continued to be a guide and explore the mountains and plains. Bridger could not read or write. But he spoke French and ten Indian languages.

He was accepted and understood by the Indians. Bridger had three Indian wives but not at the same time! He went blind in his later years and died on his farm near Kansas City in 1881.

He was once described as a plain and humble man with a 'heroic spirit'.

## 3.1 The first trailblazers?

### Mountain men and Trappers
These men earned their living by selling the skins of animals they trapped, mainly beavers. Then they sold the fur back East. They often lived like Indians and traded with them.

## The importance of the mountain men

As well as trapping animals, mountain men were also adventurers and explorers. They got to know the Sierra Nevada, the Rockies, the Plains and the land near the Pacific Ocean very well. When they went back to the East to sell their beaver skins they talked about their adventures. Sometimes their stories were printed in newspapers.

These stories encouraged other people to go West. The mountain men often helped them to plan their routes.

## The first trails

Mountain men who helped to find new routes were sometimes called pathfinders. Among them were:

- Joseph Walker who helped to set up the Santa Fe trail.
- Jedediah Smith who gave advice about the route through the Rockies.
- Jim Bridger who guided wagon trains over the Great American Desert.
- John Frémont who found and mapped out a new route over the Rockies that became known as the Oregon Trail. In 1844 the US Government printed 10,000 copies of his report and map. Many of those who read Frémont's report were encouraged to go West.

The US Government believed in manifest destiny (see page 11). It wanted to settle all the land between the Atlantic and Pacific Oceans with White Americans. This is why they helped Frémont.

▼ The trails to the Pacific coastlands.

## The great migration

The first group of settlers left the town of Independence, Missouri in 1843, a year before Frémont's map was published. About 1,000 men, women and children travelled in covered wagons to Oregon. Wagons travelled together for safety. It was a journey of 3,200 kilometres. This was the beginning of what became known as the **great migration**.

Source A

▲ *Emigrants Crossing the Plains*, painted by Albert Bierstadt in 1867. He was a German-born artist who was fascinated by the natural beauty of the West. His paintings were very popular in the 1860s with people who still lived in the East.

## Preparing for the journey

At Independence people bought covered wagons and oxen. They stocked up with food and other supplies. This was difficult as they did not know how much they would need – or how much they could carry. They had no idea how difficult it would be to cross dangerous rivers or climb mountain passes. Often their wagons were too heavily loaded. Precious family possessions sometimes had to be left at the side of the trail.

## The journey

After 'fitting out' the wagon 'train' left Independence. It crossed the Great Plains along the Platte River and rested at Fort Laramie. The Rockies had to be crossed through the South Pass. By now the wagons had travelled 1,600 kilometres. When they reached Fort Bridger they stopped again for repairs and to buy more food.

The wagons then continued their journey over the Plateaux region to Fort Hall. Here the trail divided. Some travellers turned north to Oregon; others went south to California.

## Travellers to Oregon

The wagon train continued to follow the Snake River to Fort Boise. It then crossed the Sierra Nevada and down into the Willamette valley of Oregon.

Settlers could farm here just as they had done in the East. By 1845 there were 6,000 Americans in Oregon.

## Travellers to California

The first travellers to California used the Santa Fe trail, but it was difficult. After gold was found in 1848, a new trail was opened up to Sutter's Fort near to where gold was first discovered.

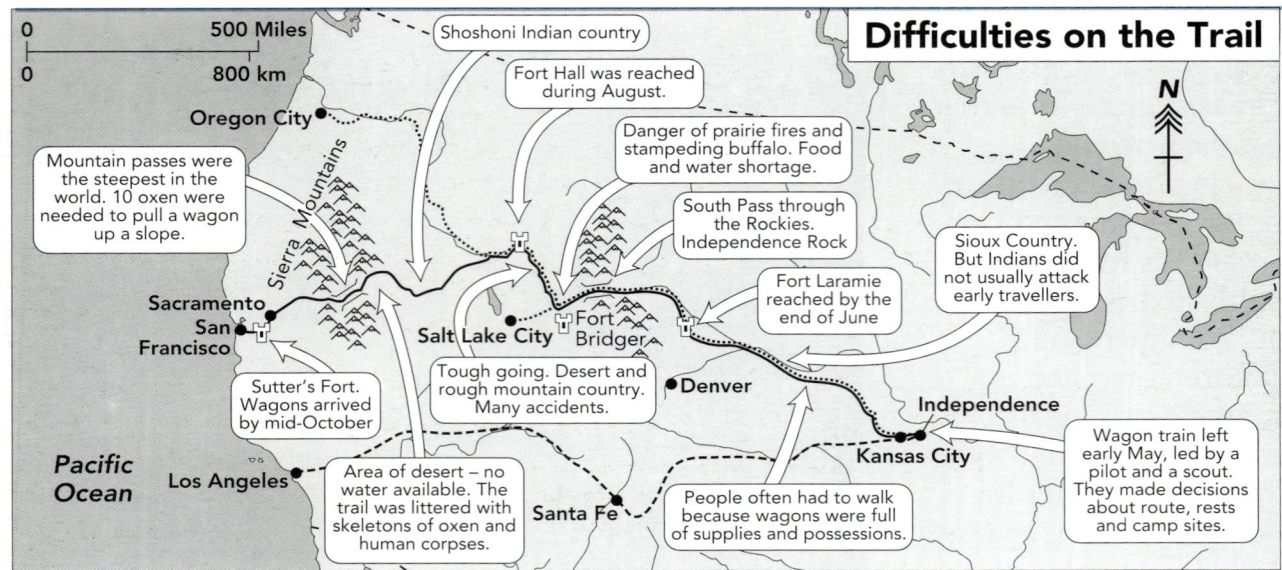

**Difficulties on the Trail**

### Did the migrants see themselves as trailblazers?

High up on the South Pass in the Rocky Mountains is a huge stone, called Independence Rock. On it are carved the names of many of the travellers who went that way. A stone mason was there to carve the names. It was obviously very important to many people to have their names recorded. Perhaps they saw themselves as trailblazers helping to bring about the destiny of the USA.

## 3.2 All that glistens – is it gold?

### Gold in California

In January 1848 James Marshall, a carpenter, was building a mill. He was working for John Sutter of Sutter's Fort. When he went to inspect the channel that had been dug for the millwheel, he saw something gleaming. The next day Sutter confirmed that it was gold.

At first it was kept a secret. But soon the news leaked out. People rushed to California to see if they could find gold. By the end of 1848, 10,000 men were digging for gold.

### The forty-niners

The forty-niners were settlers who went to California in 1849 to look for gold or to start up businesses. They travelled overland and by sea. There were soon 90,000 **prospectors** (gold diggers) looking for gold.

### Source A

Frenzy seized my soul; unbidden my legs performed entirely new movements of polka steps – I took several. Houses were too small for me to stay in . . . piles of gold rose up before me at every step, castles of marble, dazzling the eye . . . in short, I had an attack of gold fever.

▲ A San Francisco man writing about his reaction to hearing the news that gold had been discovered in California in 1848.

## Source B

The hardships of the overland route to California are unimaginable. Fear of losing animals and fear of being left in the mountains to starve and freeze to death, are things of which I may write and you may read, but are nothing to the reality.

▲ John Lloyd Stephens, a traveller and author, writing in 1849.

## Source C

I know of no country in which there is so much corruption, villainy, outlawry . . . and every variety of crime and meanness.

▲ From Hinton R. Helper, *The Land of Gold: Reality Versus Fiction*. Helper went from North Carolina to California in the late 1840s, and later wrote about his experiences of the gold rush.

## Source D

The stories that you hear are the biggest lies imaginable – the mines are a humbug. All hopes of making a fortune in California are lost sight of in 99 cases out of a 100, and the almost universal feeling is to get home. It is truly heart-rending to see the general despondency which exists among miners, and to see brave men shed tears at their hopeless condition.

▲ From a letter written by a gold prospector to his brother in 1849. It shows the poverty and desperation of the many prospectors.

## What was life really like in California?

The dreams of becoming rich soon disappeared. Only a few were lucky. There was not much gold (see Source D).

The mining camps were rough and wild. Most prospectors were under thirty years of age. They came to look for gold, intending to return home when they became rich. They did not plan to settle in California. That is why living conditions were so poor. A gold digger finding small amounts of gold could earn about $20 a day, but it cost him $18 to live. So he had no money to return home. Life became desperate.

## Prospecting for gold

Most people used the paning process (see Source E). There was very little gold in the river beds and so they were usually unlucky. Gold was mainly found underground. Digging mines was expensive. Companies from the cities in the East paid to have mines dug and provided machinery.

## Source E

▶ Panning for gold in 1849. This was the simplest method of looking for gold. Dirt was gathered in water from the river bed. The lighter dirt was shaken away showing up the gold – if there was any there.

## Problems resulting from the gold rush

The discovery of gold brought problems both for California and all the USA.

**Racism** – Gold attracted people from all over America and other parts of the world. These included Mexicans, Chinese, Indians and Blacks. White Americans thought they were better than the other people. (Remember there was still slavery in some American states.) Foreign miners had to pay taxes but American miners did not. American miners often refused to work with Chinese miners. Also, the native Indians of California were almost wiped out because of the huge number of settlers coming from the East.

**Poor living conditions** – Imagine life in a gold mining community. So many people arrived so quickly. They all hoped to make their fortune but very few did. Living conditions were very unpleasant. Miners lived in dirty, primitive tents or cabins. Fever and cholera spread rapidly.

**Problems of law and order** – Miners became bored and disappointed. They turned to gambling and heavy drinking. There was no proper system of law and order or any proper courts. Murder and claim-jumping were very common. Claim-jumping was when miners took over a mine that someone else had claimed before them. This led to fights, arguments and sometimes death.

**Vigilantes** – In some towns miners set up their own courts to deal with these problems. In some areas **vigilante** groups were started to keep law and order. These were gangs of men who decided they would punish people who broke the law, but often these vigilantes were as bad as those they were trying to punish.

### Source F

▲ An engraving showing hangings by vigilantes in San Francisco in 1851. The men being executed had been accused of starting fires in the city, and the vigilantes had taken over as the lawmen in San Francisco.

▲ The location of mining activity in the American West, 1848–74.

## THE DONNERS

The danger of pioneer travel is shown in the story of the Donner Party. The Donners were travelling with a large group of people. (People tried to travel in big groups for safety.) They were rushing to cross the Sierra Nevada mountains before the winter snows came. The mountains were dangerous at all times. In winter they were impossible to cross.

The Donners and some others decided to split from the main group and take a less well-known route that looked shorter. They were trapped by the snow.

Some of the group pressed on to try to get help. The rest made shelters by a lake. They ate all their supplies. Still help did not come. They began to die of starvation and cold. Those who lived had to eat the dead to survive until they were rescued.

## Benefits of finding gold

In spite of all the problems, the discovery of gold in California in 1848, and later in Nevada and Dakota, was an important **turning point** in these regions. This means it was a time of great change. These areas began to grow and became rich. The discovery of gold also helped the growth of the USA as a whole. There were many benefits:

- The supply of money increased. This helped to expand gold mining and other industries such as ship building.
- San Francisco grew rapidly. It soon became as important a financial centre as New York.
- It made sure that when the railway across America was built in the 1860s, it would go through California and not Oregon.
- It helped the USA to become a leading country in world trade.

## SUMMARY

▶ Mountain men and trappers were great pathfinders. Their trails were used by thousands of migrants.

▶ The 'great migration' began at Independence, Missouri in 1843.

▶ Life on the trails was hard.

▶ The Californian gold rush began in 1848.

▶ Gold in the West made California a rich state.

## 3.3 The Mormons: migrants of another sort

The pioneers who first went West were farmers and goldminers. The Mormons were also pioneers but they had a different way of living and their reasons for going were different.

The Mormons were a religious group. They all lived together as a group and shared everything.

They travelled west to escape from **persecution**. This means that their lives were being made miserable because other people did not share their beliefs. They wanted to go somewhere where they could live in peace.

### Who were the Mormons?
Their proper name was **The Church of Jesus Christ of the Latter Day Saints**. Their beliefs and way of life made them different from other Americans. The church was founded by Joseph Smith in 1830.

### Joseph Smith
Joseph Smith was born in Vermont, the son of a poor farmer. In 1823 Smith said that he had seen a vision of an angel called **Moroni**. The angel told Smith that he would help him find some golden plates. **Mormon**, father of Moroni had written scripture on the golden plates.

### The book of Mormon
Joseph Smith translated Mormon's words and wrote them down in the **Book of Mormon**. This became the Bible of the Mormons and was published in 1830. It describes how some of the Old Testament tribes of Israel migrated to America. It also tells how Jesus went to America after he rose from the dead. Eleven people were allowed to see the plates to prove that Smith was telling the truth.

▲ Joseph Smith, the founder of the Mormon church.

### Source A

**The calling of Joseph Smith**

On the evening of 21 September [1823] . . . I went to pray. Whilst I was praying, a light suddenly came into my room. The light grew brighter and brighter. It was like the middle of the day. Then a person stood at the side of my bed. He floated in the air. He wore a brilliant white robe. His whole person was very bright. He said that he was a messenger from God and that his name was Moroni. He said that God had work for me to do and that my name would be well known by all people.

▲ The calling of Joseph Smith, taken from the 'Testimony of the Prophet Joseph Smith', in the *Book of Mormon*.

## Early success
By 1831, a thousand people had joined the Mormon Church. Many Mormon **missionaries** went out to convert people. They spread Mormon ideas in America and also in Britain. Joseph Smith said that God wanted him to build a 'holy city' or **Zion** in America.

## Kirtland in Ohio
Joseph Smith chose to build his 'holy city' in Kirtland, Ohio. He went to live there in 1831. In 1833 the Mormons began to build their first temple. Even more people became Mormons. Smith also set up a bank. This was used by both Mormons and non-Mormons.

## The Mormons in trouble
But soon there were signs of trouble. The people of Kirtland felt that they were being overrun. The number of Mormons was increasing. Mormon houses were attacked and some Mormons were tarred and feathered.

## The collapse of the Mormon bank
In 1837 there was a money crisis in America. It affected Smith's bank badly. Both Mormons and non-Mormons who had money in the bank lost everything. They were all angry with Smith. The non-Mormons attacked the Mormons and drove them out of Kirtland.

## Missouri – another home?
Joseph Smith took his people to Missouri. They only stayed there for a year (1837–38) because the other settlers did not want them. Smith and the leaders were put in prison and the other Mormons left.

### Some Mormon beliefs and practices
- They owned nothing and they shared everything.
- They obeyed God completely and were His chosen people.
- As many people as possible should be made Mormons.
- A man could have more than one wife (polygamy).
- The leaders of the Mormon Church could make decisions over everyday things as well as over religion.

### Source B
As we could not join our neighbours in their midnight revels, their Sabbath breaking, horse-racing and gambling, they started at first to ridicule, then to persecute us.

Next an organized mob assembled and burned our houses, tarred and feathered, and whipped many of our brethren, and finally drove them from their houses.

These events were ignored by the government, and although we had deeds for our land and had broken no law, we could obtain no justice.

▲ Joseph Smith describes how the Mormons were treated in Missouri.

### NAUVOO
In 1843 an Englishman visited Joseph Smith's 'holy city' of Nauvoo. Later, he wrote about what he saw there.

The town was well laid out, with straight, tree-lined roads, well-built houses, shops and businesses.

There were no saloons, and no gambling dens. Instead, Nauvoo was dominated by the Mormon Temple.

## Source C

Two years ago, some two or three of these people [Mormons] appeared on the Upper Missouri and they now number 1,200 souls... flooding us with the very dregs...

Complaints have been already made of their corrupting influence on our slaves... We are told that we of this country are to be cut off and our lands taken over by them.

▲ Extract from the *Missouri Intelligencer* and Boon's *Lick Advertiser* newspapers, 10 August 1833.

## Nauvoo, Illinois 1839: early success

The Mormons were taken to Illinois by Brigham Young, the only Mormon leader who had escaped prison. When Smith left prison he was given permission by the government of Illinois to build his 'holy city'. It was named Nauvoo. The Mormons were also allowed to have their own laws and their own army. Things seemed to be going well.

## Trouble again

As the number of Mormons increased, again the non-Mormons became worried. Joseph Smith said that it was God's will that Mormons could have more than one wife (this is called polygamy). Non-Mormons were disgusted by this and many Mormons did not agree with Smith about polygamy.

By 1842 the Mormon army numbered 2,000. Then Joseph Smith said that he intended to run as President. Some Americans thought that the Mormons were going to take over the USA.

## Source D

▲ An engraving of a polygamous Mormon family. Smith claimed the practice of polygamy (having more than one wife) was the will of God. Smith had ten wives by 1843.

## Death of Joseph Smith
In June 1844 Joseph Smith and his brother were arrested. In July a group of non-Mormons attacked the prison and the brothers were shot and killed.

## Why were the Mormons hated so much?
Many people who had different religions went to settle in the American West. None seemed to be hated as much as the Mormons. Why was this?

- The number of Mormons grew very quickly. This was because the Mormons worked hard to convert Americans, Indians and ex-slaves as well as people abroad.
- Joseph Smith said that polygamy was the will of God. This was hated by non-Mormons. Joseph Smith had ten wives.
- The Mormon leaders were in charge of the Mormon religion and the everyday lives of the Mormon people. Some Americans thought that if Joseph Smith became President of the USA, then the laws of the Mormons would become the laws for everyone.
- The Mormons believed that they were the chosen people of God. They saw themselves as 'special'.
- The Mormons were very hard-working and they became successful. This made some non-Mormons jealous.

### Brigham Young: profile of a leader
*Like Joseph Smith, Brigham Young came from Vermont. He was a glazier and a carpenter and was converted to the Mormon faith in 1832. He was trusted by the Mormon leadership and allowed to take charge of a mission to Britain, where he later claimed to have converted 9,000 to the faith.*

*He gained the respect of the Mormon community when he led them out of Missouri at the time when the rest of their leaders were in prison. When Joseph Smith was murdered, Young was in Boston organizing Smith's campaign for the presidency. He returned quickly to Nauvoo and became the new leader. His influence on the future of the Mormons was enormous.*

## Crisis for the Mormons
The Mormons had been constantly persecuted. They had been forced out of Kirtland, Missouri and now Nauvoo. All Mormons did not all believe that polygamy was right. Now their leader had been murdered. Small groups of Mormons left Nauvoo. This could have been the end of the Mormon Church.

### EARLY LIFE
Brigham Young was married before he became a Mormon (in 1832). He had a wife, Marian, and two daughters, Elizabeth and Vilate. Marian died just before Young joined the Mormons.

## Where next?

At this very difficult time for the Mormons one man seemed to know what to do. This man was **Brigham Young**. He became leader of the 15,000 remaining Mormons.

Before his death Joseph Smith had realized that the Mormons would have to leave Nauvoo. He had wanted to leave the USA. In 1844 areas in the West still belonged to Mexico. Brigham Young read what some of the mountain men had written and decided to lead the Mormons to the Great Salt Lake. Preparations began in 1845.

## Brigham Young - organizer

**His Problem** – to organize a journey for 15,000 men, women and children to the Great Salt Lake. This would be a difficult and dangerous journey of about 2,250km.

**His Plan** – every family was to build wagons and prepare for the journey. In Spring 1846 persecution began again. Mormons and their houses were attacked.

So one group went ahead to set up **Winter Quarters** on the banks of the Missouri River. The advance party planted crops for food. But when the Mormon wagons arrived, many people were ill. Some died.

## Crossing the Great Plains

The most difficult part of the journey was still to come. Brigham Young prepared the Mormons.

- They were divided into groups of a hundred. Each hundred was then divided into fifties and then tens.
- Each group of ten had a captain.
- They were taught to travel in columns and put their wagons in circles at night for safety.
- The daily routine was very strict. Anyone breaking the rules was punished (see Source F).

### Source E

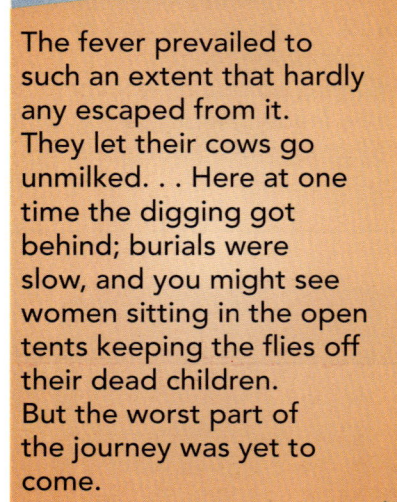

The fever prevailed to such an extent that hardly any escaped from it. They let their cows go unmilked. . . Here at one time the digging got behind; burials were slow, and you might see women sitting in the open tents keeping the flies off their dead children. But the worst part of the journey was yet to come.

▲ From an account by a US Army officer who provided medical help at one of the Mormon camps on the way to Winter Quarters.

### Source F

At 5 a.m. every man to attend prayers before he leaves his wagon. Then cooking, eating, feeding teams etc till seven o'clock, at which the camp is to move . . .

No man to be permitted to leave his wagon without permission from his officer . . . At 8.30 p.m. the bugle to be sounded at which time all to have prayers in their wagons and to retire to rest by nine p.m.

▲ From Brigham Young's orders for the journey across the Great Plains. These were in the journal (daily record) of this trip written by William Clayton, one of the travellers.

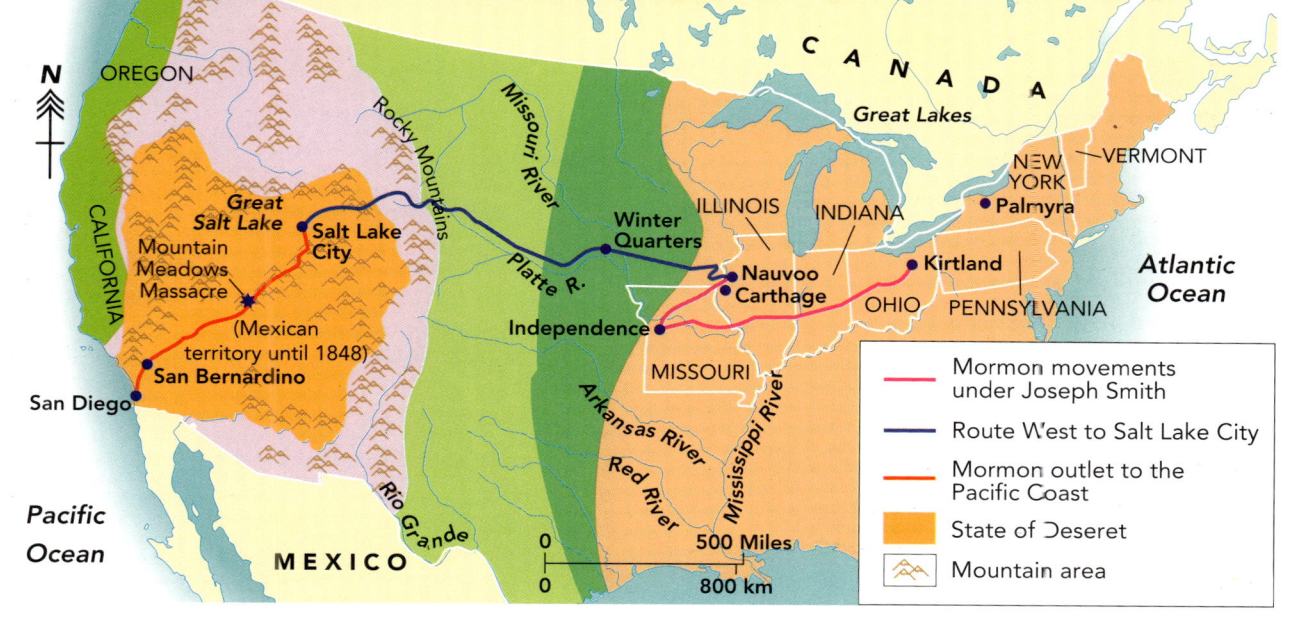

▲ The journeys of the Mormons and the state of Deseret.

## The end of the journey

The long wagon train struggled over the Plains following the Oregon Trail. They went through South Pass and found the trail to the Great Salt Lake. On 23 July Brigham Young looked over the valley and saw the chosen land.

Mormons today still celebrate 24 July as **Pioneer Day** – the day when the first group of Mormons arrived in what was to become Salt Lake City, Utah.

## Salt Lake City

Jim Bridger, the mountain man, warned Young that nothing would grow on the land near the Salt Lake. Many Mormons agreed (see Source G). Young was sure that this wilderness would become their home. The Mormons obeyed. They would build their city here.

Brigham Young would continue to be their leader. His plans, courage and determination would be needed if they were to succeed in their aim.

▶ An extract from the diary of Brigham Young's sister-in-law, Harriet, describing her first reaction to the Salt Lake valley.

### Source G

Everything looked gloomy and I felt heart sick. Weak and weary as I am, I would rather go a thousand miles farther than remain in such a desolate and forsaken spot as this.

### Brigham Young's instructions to the first Mormon settlers

- Work parties were to look for timber and fresh water supplies.
- Fields were to be planted and irrigation channels dug for water.
- Work was to begin on the 'holy city'.
- No one could own land or natural resources. Land was to be shared out but had to be farmed successfully or it would be taken back. Water was to be rationed.
- Shops, houses and other buildings were later to be allocated by Church leaders.
- One tenth of all earnings (a tithe) was to be paid to the Church.

3.3 THE MORMONS 41

## How would the Mormons survive?
The first months in the Salt Lake valley were extremely hard. In the winter many people died of cold and hunger. In the early summer grasshoppers ate the crops. These problems continued. It was not easy to settle in this area.

## Looking to the future
Brigham Young knew that two things were important if the Mormons were to survive.
1 There had to be a large number of people.
2 The Mormons had to grow all their own food and make their own clothing. They had to be **self-sufficient** so that they would not depend on the non-Mormons for anything.

He encouraged Mormons from Europe and other parts of the USA to come to the Salt Lake valley. These helped to solve both problems. When they came and settled, the population increased. They brought lots of skills with them. Some even tried to grow sugar and make their own iron.

Brigham Young set up a **Perpetual Emigration Fund** to help poor Mormons pay for the journey to the Salt Lake.

Polygamy was also encouraged. This helped the population to grow. Brigham Young had 23 wives and 49 children – to the horror of the rest of the USA.

## Ways to make the Mormons more wealthy
- In 1848, after the gold rush, Brigham Young set up supply depots and workshops. Travellers on their way to California could stop, have repairs done and buy supplies.
- Brigham Young charged tolls for travellers crossing Mormon territory.
- When the railroad was being built across the West he made sure that it passed north and south of Salt Lake City. This helped the Mormons to trade.

## An independent state?
Brigham Young hoped to make the area an independent state called Deseret. It would stretch to the California coast.

In 1848 Mexico handed over land to the USA including the Salt Lake valley. So Brigham Young then applied for Deseret to become a state of the USA. But the Government decided to make Deseret a territory. It was to be smaller in area and called Utah after the Ute Indians who lived there, not Deseret.

---

### Source H

**Some views of Brigham Young**

A devout believer, but more especially a lion-hearted man of iron will, an organizer and the founder of a commonwealth.
**Written by H. E. Bolton, Young's biographer.**

Outside observers claimed that his leadership was characterized by dictatorship, arrogance and suspicion.
**From H. S. Commager, *The West*, 1976.**

He has been the brain, the eye, the ear, the mouth and hand for the entire people.
**From a speech made at Young's funeral in 1877.**

There is a batch of governors and judges and other officials here shipped from Washington, but Brigham Young is King.
**A visitor to Utah after 1860.**

## Utah

Young became the first governor of Utah but was told that the Mormons would have to obey the laws of the USA. The Mormons refused to do this.

Government officials were sent to Utah but they were attacked. Young used a secret association called the **Danites** to defend the Mormons. He also used the Danites to defend himself from any Mormons who did not agree with him.

The US Government was afraid that there would be a war. So they said that the Mormons could live in their own way but their territory would never become a state until they stopped polygamy.

## Brigham Young's influence

When Brigham Young died in 1877 the Mormons were still unpopular. However, Salt Lake City was a prosperous city by then. There were over 100,000 Mormons in 300 settlements around Salt Lake City. The Mormons were firmly established.

### SUMMARY

- **1830** Joseph Smith wrote the *Book of Mormon* and began to gain followers.
- **1831–7** The Mormons settled in Kirtland, Ohio
- **1837–8** The Mormons were driven from Kirtland. They settled briefly in Missouri.
- **1838** The Mormons moved to Illinois and built the city of Nauvoo.
- **1843** The start of the great migration to Oregon.
- **1844** Mormon persecution in Nauvoo. Joseph Smith murdered. Brigham Young became leader.
- **1846–7** Mormons were driven from Nauvoo. They went to the Great Salt Lake.
- **1848** Mexico handed over land to the USA including the Salt Lake valley. Utah became a territory of the USA.
- **1896** Utah became a state

Many of Young's ideas such as the paying of tithes, and property belonging to everyone, still remain today. The Mormons ended polygamy in 1890. Utah became a state in 1896.

# 3.4 The Mormons after Brigham Young

When Brigham Young died, John Taylor became the Mormon leader. Taylor had emigrated from England to Canada in 1830. Under Taylor, and later leaders, the Mormon Church grew and prospered. It was still involved in all aspects of people's lives. Women's groups (like the Young Women's Mutual Improvement Association), started by Brigham Young, were carried on after his death.

Sunday Schools and weekday groups taught children religion. The Church also set up libraries, schools, colleges and universities.

Between 1900 and 1950 the Mormons spread their faith to other parts of America. They then moved on to preach in other countries. By the 1960s, there were Mormons in England, Germany, Holland and Australia.

# CHAPTER 4

# TRAINS TO CROSS A CONTINENT

On the 10 May 1869 there was a ceremony at Promontory Point in Utah. Two stretches of railway line, one starting in California in the West and the other coming from the East, were joined together. The last spike to complete the line was made of gold. The railway now ran right across the USA. People could travel from the East coast to the West coast and back.

This chapter describes how this railway was built and the effect in had on American life. But how did settlers keep in touch with their relatives, and get their supplies, before the railway was built?

**Source A**

▲ A steamboat called the *Little Eagle* on the Missouri River in Kansas.

## 4.1 What transport preceded the railways?

The settlers liked to keep in touch with their relatives back home in the East. They needed letters and supplies to be sent to them in their new homes in the west. Settlers also wanted to sell farm produce to the East.

Steamboats only travelled along main rivers. By 1846 there were 1,190 steamboats carrying mail and supplies, but they were very slow. So by 1850 faster ways of travel had to be found. The government began to pay to improve the roads.

### Why was there a need for faster transport?
- The discovery of gold in California meant that more settlers went there. So there were more letters, newspapers and supplies to be sent.
- US Army posts in the West needed food and ammunition.
- The US Government in Washington needed to send judges and other officials to settlements in the West.

### Source B

A stagecoach and team of horses preparing to leave a Wells Fargo office.

### Source C

In very cold weather do not drink alcohol when on the road; because you will freeze twice as quickly when under its influence.

Do not smoke a strong pipe inside the coach – spit on the leeward side.

Don't swear or lop over neighbours when sleeping.

Expect discomfort and some hardship.

▲ Advice to stage coach travellers in the *Omaha Herald*, 1877.

## 1 Stage coaches
The most famous stage coach was the **Wells Fargo Express**. By 1850 it was possible for passengers to travel by stage-coach from Independence, in Missouri to Salt Lake City, in Utah.

## 2 Freight wagons
These were set up to carry military supplies to army posts in 1853. Then they began to carry other supplies.

## 3 Mail coaches
John Butterfield set up an overland mail service in 1857. His coaches took letters right across America. In 1858 he had 250 coaches, 1,500 horses and 800 men. It took almost three weeks for a letter to go from the East to a settler in the West. This was still too slow!

## 4 The Pony Express
By 1869 there was a much faster way, using the Pony Express.

Young men were employed to ride between **relay stations** across the West at breakneck speed. These young men carried the mail in special saddle bags. As one rider got near the relay station the next man was ready to take the mail bags and ride to the next relay station. The company bought 500 ponies and employed 200 young men. There were 150 relay stations following the Oregon and California trails. They could cross from Missouri to Sacramento in California, in only ten days, calling at Salt Lake City.

## A dangerous and hard journey
The trails passed through rough countryside, sometimes in terrible weather. Sometimes riders were attacked by Indians. They were not allowed to swear or drink. Every rider was given a Bible, a shotgun and a rifle.

## Source D

▶ A painting by Frederic Remington of the Pony Express showing the changeover at a relay station.

## Source E

Across the endless prairie a black speck appears against the sky, and it is plain that it moves . . . In a second or two it becomes a horse and rider, growing more and more distinct – and the flutter of hooves comes faintly to the ear – another instant a whoop and a hurrah from our upper deck, a wave of the rider's hand, but no reply, and man and horse burst past our excited faces and go swinging away.

▲ The author, Mark Twain, was excited to see a Pony Express rider in action. He included this decription of the experience in his novel, *Roughing It*, first published in 1872.

## The first telegraph message

The Pony Express lasted for only two years. In October 1861 the first **telegraph** message was sent across America. Messages could be sent along telegraph wires even more quickly than the riders could take them.

## The legend of the Pony Express

These daring young men had become very popular. Many stories were told about their bravery. One story told of a rider who arrived at a relay station dead in the saddle. His body was full of Indians arrows but he was still desperately protecting the mail. Stories like this made Pony Express riders part of the romance and legend of the West.

## Source F

Young, skinny, wiry fellows, not over 18 years of age. Must be expert riders, willing to risk death daily. Orphans preferred. Wages $25 a week.

▲ An advertisement for Pony Express riders in a San Francisco newspaper in 1860.

## CALAMITY JANE

Martha Jane Cannary, called Calamity Jane (1852–1903), lived like a man. She did many different jobs, including working on the railroad.

## 4.2 How was the railway built across the USA?

In 1853 the US Government paid $150,000 for a survey to be made for possible railway routes across America. By 1860 railways had been built from the east coast to the Mississippi River.

### Why did the US Government want a railway to be built?

The US Government wanted to:

- send judges and officials to the West to keep law and order.
- share in the wealth brought by the discovery of gold in California.
- trade with China. The railway could take goods quickly to west coast ports.
- make it easier for settlers to move West. This would help 'manifest destiny' succeed.

So in 1862 Congress (the US lawmakers) passed the Pacific Railways Act. This said that a railway would be built across America.

Two companies were set up to build the railway. The Union Pacific (into the East) and the Central Pacific (into the West) were both given land and Government loans.

Government officials would pay reduced fares when they travelled on the railway. Supplies sent to Army outposts would also be sent at a reduced rate.

### What were the problems in building the Railway?

- Not enough money.
- Terrible weather – blizzards, freezing cold, blistering heat.
- Shortage of labour. Chinese and Irish workers were used.
- Difficult landscape – mountains, canyons and landslides.

**Source A**

▶ Chinese workers building a section of the railway through the Sierra Nevada mountains in 1867.

## Getting over the problems

The railway companies had to get business people to provide money to help them. It was very dangerous for the workers particularly when blasting through mountains. In 1863 about 10,000 workers were brought in from China.

The Government said it wanted the railway completed by 10 May 1869. This looked doubtful at one stage because of the Civil War (1861–5). Irish workers were also brought in and the lines joined on time at Promontory Point, Utah. The railway was **transcontinental** – it went right across the USA.

## 4.3 What impact did the railways have?

After the first transcontinental railway was finished, railway building became very popular. Four more railways were built across America as well as many branch lines. They carried passengers and goods to outlying areas.

### Some people disliked the railways
- Business people were unhappy because prices varied so much.
- Some farmers were unhappy. They thought the railway companies were more interested in making money than in providing a good service.

▶ Transport across the USA. The routes of the transcontinental railways in the last quarter of the 19th century.

- Some people were sad because the railways meant the end of the stagecoaches, freight wagons and the Pony Express.
- The Indians lost out. Railways brought new settlers who wanted Indian land. The settlers disturbed and killed the buffalo.

## Other people liked the railways

Railways made travel easier for everyone. Government officials and judges could get more quickly to new settlements. Relatives could now travel to visit settlers.

Supplies could be sent to the West much more easily. Settlers needed food, seeds and machinery. When settlers made money, they wanted to buy things for their homes. Farm products from the West could be taken more quickly by rail to be sold in other parts of America.

## Railways and the industrial revolution

At the same time that railways were being built, the USA was having an industrial revolution. Coal and other raw materials could now be taken by rail to factories. The finished goods were taken by rail (from factories) to be sold in different parts of America Railways helped to make the USA become the world's most important industrial country by 1890. They helped to increase trade at home and abroad and make the USA wealthy.

## Settlers on the Great Plains

Thousands of new settlers were able to use the railways to travel West. In the next two chapters we will look at two groups of people who used the railways. They came to live on the Plains during the 1860s – the cattlemen and the homesteaders.

### SUMMARY

- ▶ Steamboats on main rivers carried people and goods.
- ▶ **1850–1** Wells Fargo stagecoaches were introduced.
- ▶ **1853** Freight wagons carried goods. The US Government paid for a survey of possible railway routes across America.
- ▶ **1857** Overland mail service set up.
- ▶ **1860** The Pony Express was started.
- ▶ **1861** Telegraph messages could be sent across America.
- ▶ **1862** Pacific Railway Act passed. Work began on the transcontinental railway.
- ▶ **1869** Railway completed.

### RAILWAY EXPANSION

The figures below show how railways expanded and how government policies helped this.

**Growth of railway milage, 1850–90**

1850: 9,021 miles
1890: 166,703 miles

**Government and state land grants to railway companies**

1856–71: 180,233,966 acres (at about $5 an acre)

**Government loans to railway companies, 1861**

$16,000 per mile on flat land.
$32,000 per mile in mountain foothills.
$48,000 per mile in mountains.

CHAPTER 5

# CATTLEMEN AND COWBOYS

**Source A**

▲ Texas Longhorns. These were a very sturdy breed of cattle that could survive by themselves in all kinds of weather conditions on the trail and on the Plains. This painting by Frank Reaugh is called *The Herd*.

## A change in attitude

In the 1860s cattlemen from the South started to set up ranches on the Great Plains. They found that the area which had been called the Great American Desert by the early settlers was good for cattle ranching. The cattlemen sold their Longhorn cattle for beef.

From 1867 to the 1880s the demand for beef increased. This was called the 'beef bonanza' and it made many cattlemen rich.

It was the men who worked for the cattlemen, the cowboys, who became famous. From 1867 until the 1880s was the era of the cowboys.

## 5.1 How did the cattle industry begin?

### Cattle ranching in Texas

There had been cattle ranching in Texas since the early 19th century.

At first the ranches in Texas were quite small. They had no fences and the Texas Longhorn cattle were allowed to wander freely on the **open range**. They were branded with the mark of their owner so they could be recognized.

### More cattle in Texas

In 1861 many Texan ranchers went to fight in the Civil War. They had to leave their ranches and their cattle ran wild.

When they returned home in 1865, they found that their cattle had survived and had continued to breed. By now there were about five million Longhorns in Texas.

## Demand for beef in the North

At the end of the Civil War the growing industrial cities of the north, such as Chicago, needed as much beef as they could get. If Texan ranchers could get cattle to these cities they could make good profits. They could get ten times as much for their cattle if they sold them to markets in the North.

Cattlemen realized that if they could get their cattle to the railway then they could reach the markets of the North. Ranchers rounded up their cattle and hired cowboys to take them on the long trail to the railhead. Many cowboys used the Sedalia/Shawnee trail. At Sedalia, the cattle were loaded onto trains for St Louis and Chicago.

## 5.2 Who was behind the 'beef bonanza'?

### 1 Joseph McCoy

Joseph McCoy is said to have started the 'beef bonanza' (the great increase in the beef trade). He was a cattle trader in Chicago. He wanted to make Chicago the centre of the meat trade.

### Problems on the Sedalia/Shawnee Trail

The cowboys using the Sedalia/Shawnee Trail had run into problems. They were attacked by farmers in Kansas. The farmers did not want cattle crossing their land because the Longhorns carried a tick (a kind of insect) that did not harm them, but killed other animals. There were also problems with rustlers and robbers.

### McCoy's idea

Joseph McCoy knew that the railway companies wanted more business. The Kansas Pacific Railway agreed to take its new railway past a village which was given the name Abilene. It grew into one of the first **cow towns**. Abilene was built up by McCoy as a place where cowboys could hand over cattle to northern buyers. McCoy paid for the building of a hotel, a stockyard for 3,000 cattle, an office and a bank. He promised Texan ranchers that they would get good prices for their cattle in Abilene.

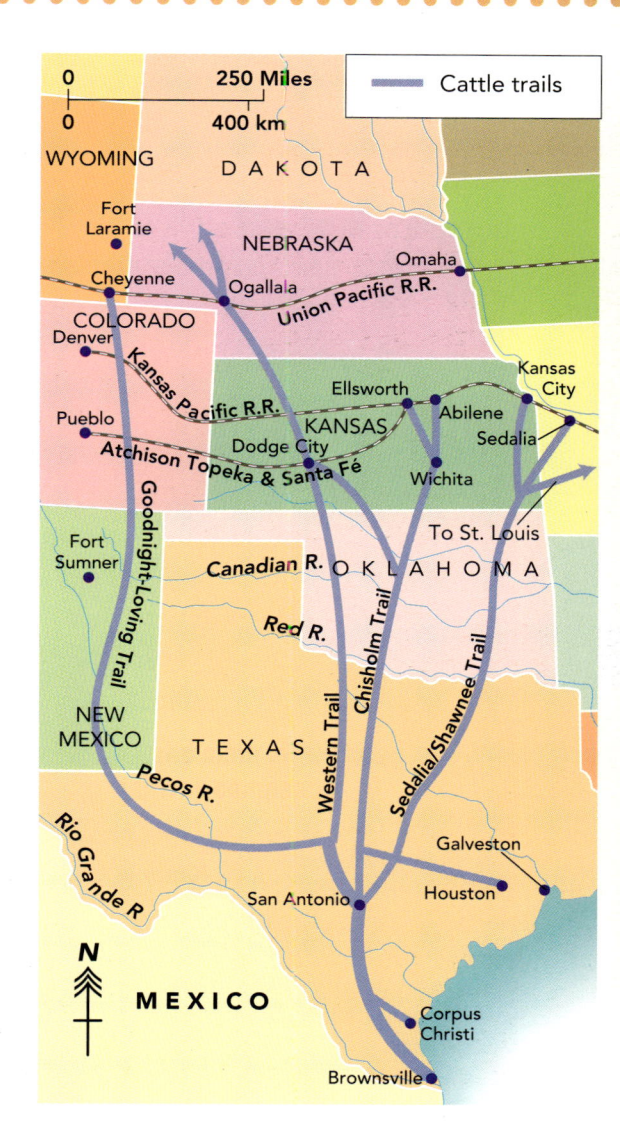

▲ **Cattle trails across the Great Plains.**

## Source A

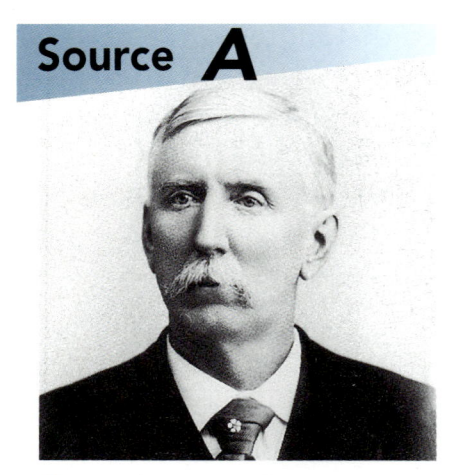

▲ Joseph McCoy, Chicago cattle dealer.

## Source B

▲ Charles Goodnight.

▶ The cow town of Abilene, Kansas in 1879. Between 1867 and 1880 half the cattle transported along the Kansas Pacific Railway came up the Chisholm Trail, and departed for the eastern cities from Abilene, Ellsworth and Dodge City.

## The 'Real McCoy'

By the end of 1867, 35,000 head of cattle had been driven along the Chisholm Trail to Abilene. The 'beef bonanza' had begun. McCoy was seen to be a man who kept his word. In 1868 one cattleman bought 600 head of cattle in Texas for $5,400 and sold them in Abilene for $16,800.

Today people sometimes use the phrase 'the real McCoy'! It means that it is the real thing, the best of its kind. It is thought that this saying comes from Joseph McCoy and the way he set up Abilene as a cow town.

## 2 Charles Goodnight

Another man who helped to make the 'beef bonanza' was Charles Goodnight. He grew up on a farm in Texas and went into the cattle business. Before he left to fight in the Civil War he owned 180 cattle. When he returned he had 5,000 cattle!

He decided to sell his cattle to the US Government who needed meat for the Army and to feed the Indians. He teamed up with another rancher called **Oliver Loving**. They tried a new trail. It went through Indian territory where water was scarce but they made a huge profit. They opened the new trail and found new markets.

## Source C

## Ranching on the plains

In the 1870s some cattlemen, who were tired of the dangers and difficulties of the long drives from Texas, began to set up ranches on the Great Plains. This meant they only had a short journey to the railhead. There was plenty of grass so the Longhorns could graze there as easily as in Texas.

## 3 John Iliff

Another person who helped the 'beef bonanza' to develop was John Iliff who started ranching on the **Great Plains**. Iliff began as a gold miner in Colorado in 1859. Then he opened a store on the Oregon Trail. Finally he began to buy cattle and bought his first Longhorns from Charles Goodnight.

Iliff found another market for beef. He sold it to the rail companies to feed their construction gangs who were building the transcontinental railway in 1867. He also got Government contracts to supply meat to Indians on reservations. Iliff began experimenting to improve the quality of beef. He began cross-breeding his Longhorn cattle with English cows. These produced more meat and milk than the Longhorns.

### Source D

Dudley and John W. Snyder promise to buy 15,000 head of steers [young male cattle] of the ages of two and three years next spring, and to drive the cattle to Colorado to John Iliff . . . in July 1878. John Iliff agrees to pay sixteen dollars per head for the three-year-old steers and twelve dollars for the two-year-olds per head.

▲ An extract from a contract to buy cattle from Texas cattlemen.

### Source E

. . . to be delivered on the Denver Pacific Railroad, the beef, flour, potatoes, cabbage, turnips, onions, oats, corn and hay required by the track-laying forces during the construction of the said road.

▲ Extract from a beef contract won by John Iliff in 1869.

### Source F

◀ John Iliff.

### Source G

| State/Territory | Cattle 1860 | Cattle 1880 |
|---|---|---|
| Kansas | 93,455 | 1,533,133 |
| Nebraska | 37,197 | 1,113,247 |
| Colorado | none | 791,492 |
| Wyoming | none | 521,213 |

▲ Figures for the cattle industry on the northern Plains. In only twenty years the increase was enormous.

### JESSE CHISHOLM

Not much is known about Jesse Chisholm, who was famous for blazing the Chisholm Trail. He was the son of a Scotsman and an Indian.

Chisholm worked as a trader and a scout. Indians and white settlers both trusted him.

## 5.3 Who were the cowboys?

Cowboys worked in Texas and on the Great Plains from about 1867 until the 1880s looking after the cattle. Few Americans who lived in the eastern states ever saw a real cowboy, but they thought they knew all about them. Cowboys were seen as skilful and glamorous, brave, daring and heroic.

### How did the Americans in the East know all this?

They went to see Buffalo Bill Cody's travelling Wild West shows in which so-called cowboys performed clever and daring acts. They read magazines like *Harper's Weekly* which included articles about cowboys.

### What were the cowboys really like?

They were mostly young men, rarely married. Many were Black and had been slaves, some were ex-soldiers who had fought in the Civil War and some were Indians. Some were even criminals on the run.

Cowboys were poorly paid but they enjoyed the freedom of riding the range. They lived in very basic bunk houses when at the ranch. They could lose their jobs for swearing, drinking or gambling. Their clothing was tough and hardwearing – just right for the job.

### Source A

◀ A sculpture in bronze by Frederic Remington (1902) called *Coming through the Rye*. It shows a group of cowboys riding into town. Remington was fascinated by the courage, speed and skill of the cowboy.

54 CHAPTER 5 CATTLEMEN AND COWBOYS

'The bandana. The handkerchief (usually red) which was worn around the neck, and for use as a mask. When the cowboy rode along behind the herd of cattle, he pulled the handkerchief up over his nose and mouth to protect him from the dust'.

'The hat (stetson) was made of felt. The broad brim protected the wearer from the sun and was an umbrella in rainy weather. In winter it could be pulled down over the ears and tied – giving protection from frostbite'.

'The saddle was the cowboy's throne – its bumps and contours grew to fit the owner's body. A man might gamble away his money, horse or chaps, but he would put his saddle on his back and return home on foot'.

A lariat or lasso.

'The "chaps" were an overgarment like a pair of trousers with a cut-out seat. Many were made of the shaggy skin of a bear, goat or sheep. They were also to withstand the thorny vegetation, the cutting north wind, and to protect the legs from chafing during a long ride and in the case of a fall'.

'All cowboys wore high heeled boots. The heel and arch were made so that the foot and leg were comfortable when riding. Spurs were worn at all times'.

▲ The cowboy – his clothing and equipment. Extracts from *The Long Drive* by Everett Dick.

## Source B

Some cowboys were rotten. John Hardin was one of them . . . John Wesley Hardin was the son of a Methodist preacher . . . While driving 1,200 Longhorns on the Chisholm Trail toward Abilene, he shot two Indians, one for demanding a toll. A little further along the trail he got into a row with some Mexican cowhands. He settled that sqabble by spilling the blood of five of them all over the prairie.

▲ Royal B. Hassrick, *The American West*, 1975. The cowboy's way of life was useful to those who wanted to avoid the law!

## Source C

Most cowboys were Southerners and they were a wild, reckless bunch. They wore wide-brimmed beaver hats, black or brown with a low crown, fancy shirts, high heeled boots, and a waistcoat.

▲ A description of a cowboy's dress by a cowboy, 'Teddy Blue'.

# The life of the cowboy

The Longhorns grazed on the open range so the cowboy spent hours in the saddle, roaming the plains. His days were long. His work was often hard and dangerous.

**Winter** was the most boring time of the year. In pairs, cowboys had to patrol the grazing land and make sure the cattle were safe in the snow. They had to watch for wild animals. When the snow melted they had to rescue cattle that sank in the mud.

In the **spring** the cowboys had to round up the cattle. The young calves had to be separated and branded.

In the **summer** the cowboys had to round up the cattle again and separate those cattle to be driven north on the long drive.

**Rounding up and branding** could take up to three months. Cowboys from several ranches usually joined together for this. They looked for their own brand. Usually the calves stayed close to their mothers so it was not difficult to find new stock. The cowboy had to lasso the young animal. It was then branded with a red hot branding iron. During the round up and branding the cowboys lived in camps out on the range. At the centre of the camp was the chuck wagon where the cook prepared the meals.
Rounding up the cattle was very dangerous. They had roamed freely on the range so they were like wild animals. Their long horns made it more difficult for the cowboys to catch them.

**Brands**

▶ Robin May, *History of the American West*, 1984.

## Source D

▲ *Roping a Steer* (young male) by Charles Russell. Russell worked as a cowboy for a time on a ranch in Montana.

## Source E

The best paid job out of season was killing wolves. The best method was to track a wolf to its lair when it was slowed down by food. Then one cowboy crawled into the lair holding a candle and a six gun. As the gun's explosion often blew the candle out, the job was not for the nervous.

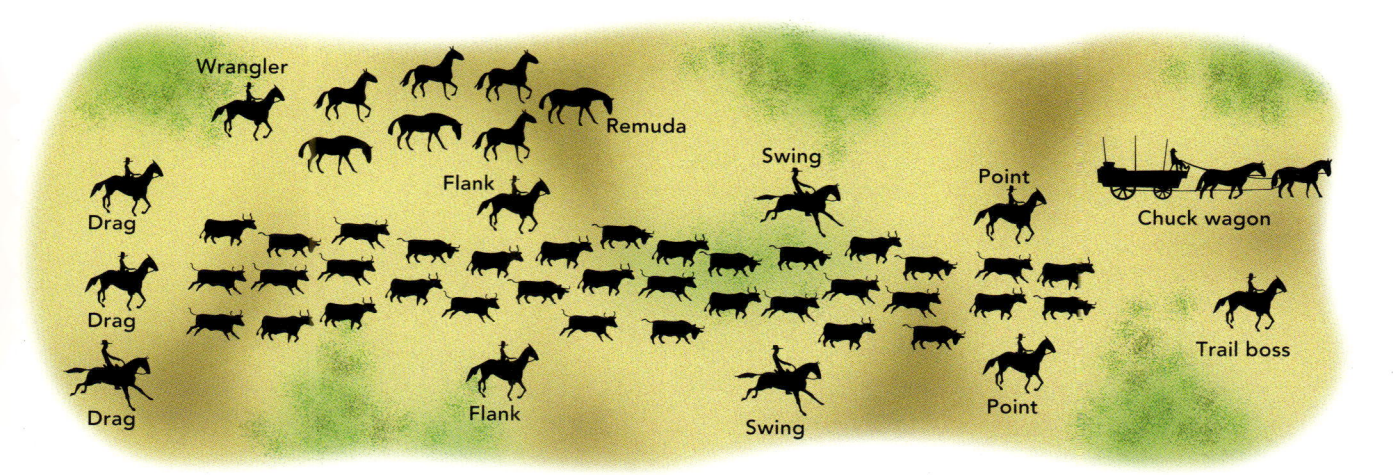

▲ The long drive. After branding, the cattle to be sold had to be taken to the railhead. This diagram shows how the cowboys were organized on the drive.

## The long drive

From 1866 until the mid 1890s the cowboys had to drive the cattle from Texas to the cow towns on the railway. This could take up to two months.

The average herd was made up of about 2–3,000 head of cattle, but herds could be as small as 600.

The cowboy had a great responsibility to get all the cattle safely to the cow town. If he lost any of the cattle, the rancher would lose money.

So the long drive was a challenge for all cowboys. Their day began at 4.00 a.m. and ended after dark. Even then cowboys had to stand on guard some time during the night.

The cowboys worked as a team but each had his own job to do (see the diagram at the top of the page):

- The **trail boss** was in charge. He got up at 3.30 a.m. and made sure there was enough food before waking the men. He gave orders, checked the herd and then rode ahead to find water. He decided where the camp would be made and generally took care of the men. He rode at the front of the herd.
- The **pointers** were also experienced riders. They led the herd when the trail boss went ahead to look for water or a camp.
- The **swing** and **flank** men rode at the side to keep the herd together.
- The **drag** men were at the back. This was the worst job because they were covered in dust from the herd in front.

The **wranglers** were the youngest and most inexperienced cowboys on the drive. They carried messages up and down the line and looked after the **remuda**, the spare horses.

## What were the difficulties of the long drive?

**Stampedes**
The slightest sound could make the cattle stampede especially at the start of the long drive when they were restless. They could stampede several times in one night. Stampedes made cattle lose weight and this lowered their value. Stopping a stampede was very dangerous. Cowboys tried to drive the cattle into a circle to slow them down.

**Weather**
Blistering hot winds and torrential rain and hailstones often made conditions unpleasant.

**Rivers**
Crossing rivers was often dangerous, especially if they were swollen by rain or there were quicksands.

**Rustlers**
These were animal thieves who were a danger – especially when the herd got nearer the railway. They stole cattle and changed the brand.

**Settlers**
The farmers in Kansas did not like Longhorns crossing their land. Other settlers complained that the herds damaged their crops. (Before 1874 land was not fenced off.)

**Indians**
These sometimes charged tolls for the herd to cross their land. Sometimes they caused the herd to stampede.

### Source F

This steer leaped into the air, hit the ground with a heavy thud, and gave a grunt that sounded like that of a hog. That was the signal. The whole herd was up and going – and heading right for me. My horse gave a lunge, jerked loose from me, and was away. I barely had time to climb an oak tree. The cattle went by like a hurricane, hitting the tree with their horns. It took us all night to round them up . . . next morning we found ourselves six miles from camp.

▲ Charles Goodnight describing his experience of a stampede on the long drive (undated).

▼ This painting by Frederic Remington shows Longhorns being stampeded by a flash of lightning.

### Source G

58 CHAPTER 5 CATTLEMEN AND COWBOYS

## What happened at the end of the trail?

When the herd was near to the cow town the cattle were allowed to graze to fatten them up before meeting the dealer. Then the cowboys rode through the town with their herd, firing their guns. Now they would get their reward! There were plenty of places for cowboys to spend their money. The cow towns were full of saloons, gambling houses and brothels. There were brawls, gunfights and drunkenness. By the late 1870s families were settling in cow towns. Women and children helped to calm things down. In 1872 Abilene banned cowboys, so other cow towns then became the journey's end.

"DANCE-HOUSE."

### Source H

The Indians would stampede our horses and try to get away with them. The friendly ones would run them off at night and come back the next day to get a reward for returning them. . .

The boys took delight in doing everything they could to provoke settlers. The settlers paid us back with interest by harrassing us in every way they. The boss was arrested twice in one day for trespassing.

▲ Bill Poage, a cowboy on a long drive, describes some of the problems of the trail.

### Source I

The bar-room, the theater, the gambling room, the bawdy house, the dance house. Such is the manner in which the cowboy spends his hard-earned dollars.

▲ Joseph McCoy describing the activities of cowboys in Abilene.

### ANN WILLIS

Ann Willis (born 1878) was the daughter of a small cattle rancher. When she inherited the ranch, she supported the small ranchers against large cattle companies.

# 5.4 Why did the cattle trade rise and fall?

## The boom years

The cattle trade boomed from 1867 until the early 1880s. New refrigerated railway carriages meant that cattle could now be slaughtered before being transported to the cities. So even larger quantities of beef could be moved. Fortune hunters from Britain and Europe went to the USA. These included counts and barons who wanted to buy ranches and make money.

## Source A

◀ **Cattle barons.** These large ranch owners formed the Prairie Cattle Company in 1885, which owned over 150,000 cattle. Big companies like this helped the cattlemen to make more money.

## Why did the beef boom end?

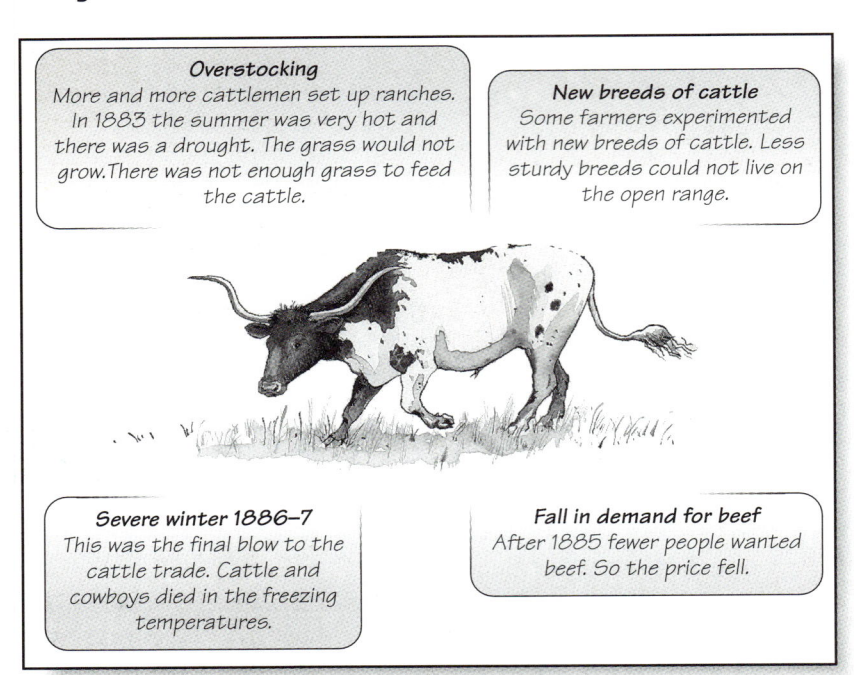

**Overstocking**
More and more cattlemen set up ranches. In 1883 the summer was very hot and there was a drought. The grass would not grow. There was not enough grass to feed the cattle.

**New breeds of cattle**
Some farmers experimented with new breeds of cattle. Less sturdy breeds could not live on the open range.

**Severe winter 1886–7**
This was the final blow to the cattle trade. Cattle and cowboys died in the freezing temperatures.

**Fall in demand for beef**
After 1885 fewer people wanted beef. So the price fell.

*The windpump* used the strong winds to power a pump which would draw water from underground. This meant that ranches no longer had to be near water.

*Barbed wire* was invented by J. F. Glidden in 1874. This meant that large areas of land could be fenced cheaply.

## A new approach

It seemed a good idea to have smaller units instead of the open range. Small amounts of better quality beef could be produced. But animals would need fencing in and water to drink.

Two new inventions made ranching possible, the windpump and barbed wire.

## The changing role of the cowboy

The role of the cowboy changed a great deal when the open range became smaller fenced ranches. There were no long drives because many ranches were on the Plains and were nearer to the railway. Round-ups were much smaller, so fewer cowboys were needed. Jobs now included mending the fences and windpumps.

The free and wild age of the cowboy was over – except in the Wild West Shows and Hollywood films. Cowboys had become part of the legend of the West.

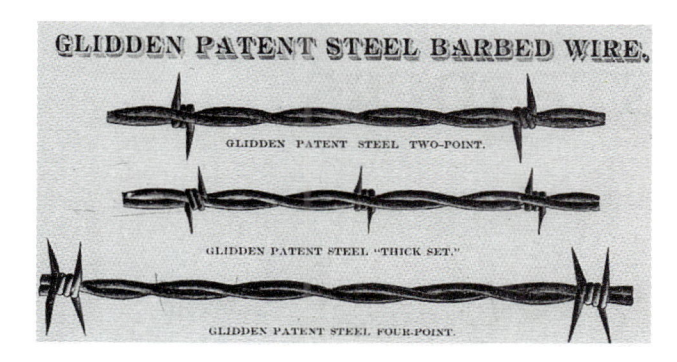

**Source B**

▲ *The Fall of the Cowboy* by Frederic Remington.

### SUMMARY

▶ **1861–5** American Civil War.

▶ **1867–1880s** 'The Beef Bonanza' pushed along by McCoy, Goodnight, Loving and Iliff.

▶ **1886–7** A very severe winter led to smaller ranches which had barbed wire fences and wind pumps. This brought the end of the cowboy era.

## 5.5 From high plains to Hollywood

So what happened to the legendary cowboy?

When his days on the Plains came to an end, Americans did not want to let go of the legend. The cowboy was taken over by Hollywood film-makers. They changed him to suit themselves.

In the 1920s and '30s the cowboy was shown as a well-dressed, handsome hero. He was ready to support any good cause and was quick on the draw. More 'realistic' films began with 'Red River', made in 1948 and starring John Wayne. This film showed the problems of a cowboy's life – long drives, stampedes, cattle rustling.

CHAPTER 6

# HOMESTEADERS ON THE PLAINS

## A change in attitude
The first settlers crossed the Great Plains as quickly as possible. They called this area the Great American Desert because the land was not good for farming. They did not want to live there.

By the 1850s and 1860 this attitude was starting to change. Some families had settled on the Low Plains (see map). They were farmers, but we usually call them **homesteaders**. By the 1880s families were even setting up homesteads (farms) on the High Plains.

So the homesteaders proved that it was possible to farm on the Great Plains, but it was still very difficult.

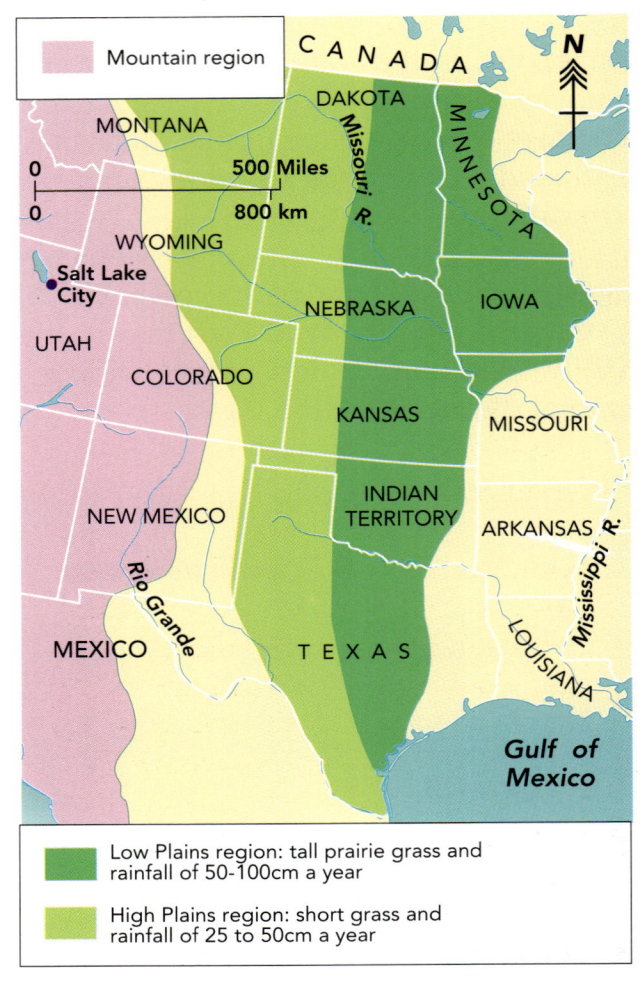

Low Plains region: tall prairie grass and rainfall of 50-100cm a year
High Plains region: short grass and rainfall of 25 to 50cm a year

▲ The areas of the Plains settled between 1860 and 1890.

## 6.1 What made the homesteaders go West?

### Where did they come from?
1 Black families came from the southern and eastern states. After the Civil War ended in 1865 the slaves were given their freedom. Some left the South to begin new lives on the Plains as homesteaders.
2 White settlers also came from the eastern states.
3 Settlers also came from abroad. They came from England, Ireland and other parts of Europe.

### Source A
The number of foreign-born immigrants on the Plains 1860–80

(% of total population)
Kansas     13 %
Nebraska   20 %
Dakota     32 %

## How did they get there?
In the 1850s the first homesteaders travelled in covered wagons. When the railways were built in the 1860s, homesteaders began to travel much more by rail.

Unlike the cowboys, almost all the homesteaders travelled West in families. The women and children helped to make the settlements on the Plains more law abiding.

## What attracted the homesteaders to the Great Plains?
The homesteaders moved West for many different reasons.

- Some had already moved near the Mississippi River. There were many people there, and not much land for sale. So they moved further west. The family of Laura Ingalls Wilder, who wrote *The Little House on the Prairie* stories, did this.
- Some went to the Plains because they were very poor. Many Irish people fit into this group.
- Some, like the Jews and Russians, were escaping from religious persecution.
- Others went because they wanted adventure.
- Some moved to join their relatives who had settled in the West.
- Magazine and newspaper articles sometimes encouraged settlers to move west.

## Who persuaded settlers to go to the Great Plains?
1 **Officials** in some territories on the Great Plains tried to persuade settlers to come to settle in their areas. These officials wanted to have more people living in their territory.

This would mean that larger towns would be built. More people meant that money would come into the territory. But most important, when a territory had 60,000 people it could apply to be a full state of the USA.

### Source C
I saw vast areas of unimproved land. We saw land before us, land behind us, land at the right hand, land at the left hand . . . oceans of land all ready for the plough, good as the best in America, and yet lying without occupants.

▲ The editor of the *Kansas Farmer* wrote this after a journey in the West in 1867.

### Source B
Ma, you can see just as far as you can please and almost every foot in sight can be ploughed.

▲ An extract from a letter, written in 1875, by a young settler in Nebraska to his mother back in the East.

### Source D
Our land is so fertile we can raise huge herds of cattle and grow large crops of corn, wheat, oats, rye, barley, buckwheat, potatoes, melons, fruits and vegetables. This shows our country can support a big population.

▲ An official from Dakota in 1869 encouraging immigration there by making extravagant claims for the fertility of the land.

### Source E

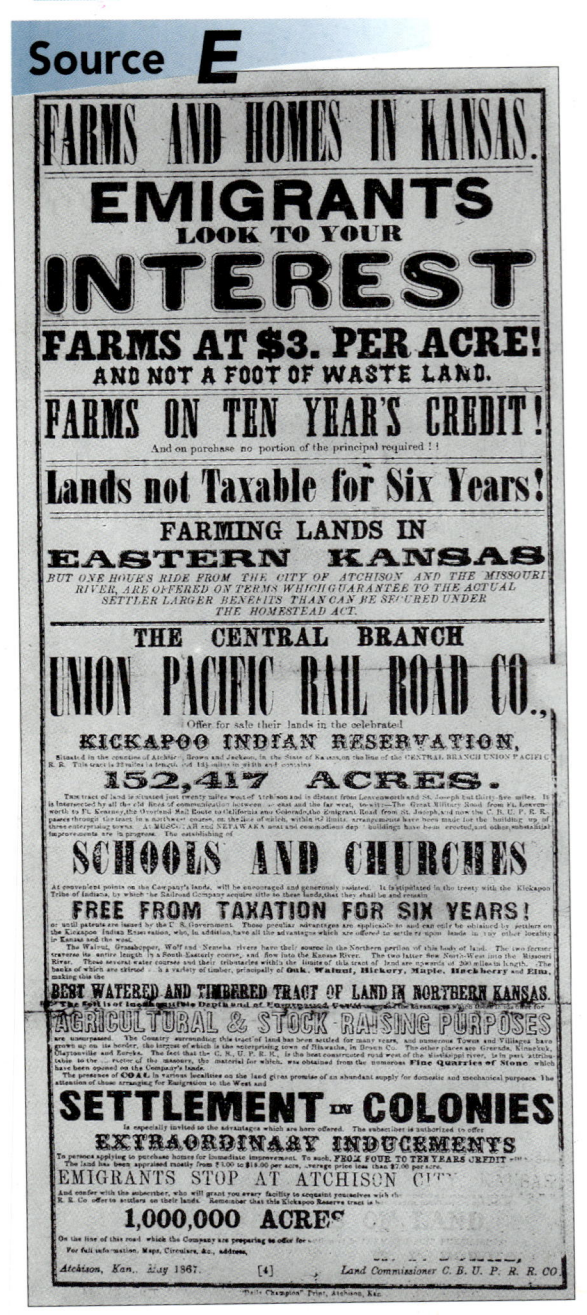

**FARMS AND HOMES IN KANSAS.**
**EMIGRANTS LOOK TO YOUR INTEREST**
**FARMS AT $3. PER ACRE!**
AND NOT A FOOT OF WASTE LAND.
**FARMS ON TEN YEAR'S CREDIT!**
And on purchase no portion of the principal required !!
**Lands not Taxable for Six Years!**
FARMING LANDS IN
**EASTERN KANSAS**
BUT ONE HOUR'S RIDE FROM THE CITY OF ATCHISON AND THE MISSOURI RIVER, ARE OFFERED ON TERMS WHICH GUARANTEE TO THE ACTUAL SETTLER LARGER BENEFITS THAN CAN BE SECURED UNDER THE HOMESTEAD ACT.

THE CENTRAL BRANCH
**UNION PACIFIC RAIL ROAD CO.,**
Offer for sale their lands in the celebrated
**KICKAPOO INDIAN RESERVATION,**
**152,417 ACRES.**

**SCHOOLS AND CHURCHES**
**FREE FROM TAXATION FOR SIX YEARS!**

**BEST WATERED AND TIMBERED TRACT OF LAND IN NORTHERN KANSAS.**
**AGRICULTURAL & STOCK-RAISING PURPOSES**

**SETTLEMENT IN COLONIES**
**EXTRAORDINARY INDUCEMENTS**
EMIGRANTS STOP AT ATCHISON CITY
**1,000,000 ACRES**

Atchison, Kan., May 1867. Land Commissioners C.B.U.P.R.R CO

▲ A Union Pacific railway advertisement offering cheap land and loans.

---

This meant there would be new and important jobs for the officials. So some officials worked hard to attract new settlers.

2 **The railway companies** also wanted to attract new settlers. They needed people to travel on the railways. The settlers would need regular supplies such as timber, seed, farm machinery. This would increase the business of the railways. The railway companies also had land which had been given to them by the Government. The railway companies needed to sell this land, in order to build more railway track. So the railway companies, as well as the officials in the territories, advertised in America and abroad. To encourage settlers to come they offered them loans which could be paid back over a number of years.

In 1875 the Santa Fe Railway invited 225 newspaper editors from the USA and abroad to visit the West at the company's expense. In 1882 half a million posters were translated into Swedish, Dutch, Danish and Norwegian. They advertised the 'good life' in the West. It really was quite a publicity campaign!

3 **The Government** was keen for people to move west. In the 1860s the Great Plains was the biggest area of land in the USA not occupied by white American settlers. The Government wanted to change this. So they offered the **land free of charge** so that poor people had a chance to become landowners in the West, as well as richer people. This would help manifest destiny happen – white Americans occupying all the land from the Atlantic Ocean to the Pacific Ocean.

## How did settlers get free land?

Settlers were able to buy land cheaply from the railway companies. Prices varied from $2.25 to $10 per acre. An Act of 1841 allowed settlers to buy 160 acres of land at the even lower price of $1.25 per acre. Finally, in 1862 the US Government set aside land in Kansas, Nebraska and Dakota and passed the **Homestead Act**. Under the Act, this land was divided into plots of 160 acres. Settlers were able to have a plot free of charge as long as they built a house and lived there for five years.

In 1873 the Government passed the **Timber and Culture Act**. This said that settlers could have a further 160 acres of free land as long as they planted trees on at least 40 acres.

## What was wrong with the Homestead Act?

Some settlers said that 160 acres of land was too little to make enough money to support their families. This may well have been true in some parts of the High Plains where it was drier and the land was not as fertile. Many settlers found that land like this was better for rearing cattle or sheep.

The Act was meant to help poorer people. But some land speculators took advantage and bought up large amounts of land. They then resold the land at a higher price. This was not what the Government had planned.

## What was good about the Homestead Act?

When the Act was passed in 1862 it seemed unlikely that people would live on the High Plains. So, for settlers on the eastern edge of the Plains, 160 acres seemed enough land. At that time the homesteaders could only afford simple tools. To farm more than 160 acres they would have needed better and more expensive machinery.

After 1873 homesteaders could have more land under the Timber and Culture Act. In 1877 the **Desert Land Act** allowed homesteaders to buy 640 acres of land in areas where rainfall was low.

So, although the Homestead Act was not perfect, it was very important in encouraging homesteaders to settle on the Plains. Altogether, it made 2.5 million acres of land available for homesteaders. In the early 1870s thousands of homesteaders were able to settle on free land. In 1871–2 in Kansas, 9,000 claims for land were made. This rose to 43,000 in 1885–7.

### SUMMARY

- The first homesteaders settled on the Plains in the 1850s.
- The Homestead Act of 1862 gave settlers 160 acres of free land.
- The Desert Land Act of 1877 made more land available in dry areas.
- In the 1870s the territories and railway companies advertised widely to encourage settlers to move West.

## 6.2 What was life like on the Plains?

So the homesteaders travelled to their new land full of excitement and hope. They had read the wonderful adverts and promises about the land where everything would grow.

Farmers from the eastern states had brought the seed and farming tools they had used there. They expected to carry on as they had done before.

They got a shock when they arrived and started to work. The seeds would not grow and their farming tools were not suitable. They were on the Great Plains now and things were very different.

### Source A

▲ A homesteader family outside its sod dug-out in 1892. It was built using bricks of living turf.

### What were the problems for the farmers?

*Prairie fires*
Fires were spread by the wind. They could destroy all crops.

*Grasshopper plagues*
Sometimes swarms were so thick that they stopped trains on the Union Pacific Railway. A plague of grasshoppers could eat all the crops. Families were left with no money to buy more seed or even food.

*The weather*
Often howling winds, but scorching hot in summer. Blizzards, hailstorms and torrential rain sometimes. Often periods of drought.

*No fencing to protect crops*
No money or wood for fencing. Crops were destroyed by wild animals or cattle.

*Very few trees*
Homes had to be built out of the hard-baked prairie earth.

*Lack of water*
Not enough for wheat to grow. The hard soil was baked by the hot sun, so it was very difficult to plough.

## Source B

The grasshoppers came upon us in untold millions, in clouds upon clouds, until their fluttering wings looked like a sweeping snowstorm in the heavens, until their dark bodies covered everything green upon the earth. In a few hours many fields that had hung so thick with long ears of maize were stripped of their value and left only a forest of bare yellow stalks.

▲ The editor of the *Wichita Eagle*, describing the effects of a grasshopper plague in the 1870s.

## WOMEN GO WEST

Life was hard for women homesteaders. But they were not the only women trying to make a life 'out West'. Women went West (usually with their husbands) to open shops, set up churches, even run saloons.

Most of the women who went West on their own went as entertainers on tour. One of the most famous of these was Lola Montez (a European dancer and singer who toured the West in 1851).

# 6.3 A tough life for women

Women had a hard time living on the Plains. The sod houses were impossible to keep clean. They were full of vermin and insects. They were dusty in dry weather and dripped with water during storms. They had no toilets and there was no clean running water. The good thing about them was that they could not be destroyed by prairie fires. There was a lot of illness because of the dirty conditions, and very few doctors. Mothers had to use their own cures. Warmed up urine was thought to be a cure for earache! Children often died from diseases like diphtheria. Many women died in childbirth.

## Source A

▲ Part of the daily life of a housewife on the Plains. This woman has collected cow or buffalo dung for fuel.

## Source B

I have fought bedbugs and fleas all summer, scrubbed rough plank floors and mingled my tears with the suds.

▲ A comment by a settler, Mrs Henry Gray to Cora Beach, a writer in *Women of Wyoming* in the late 1870s.

## Source C

It was not wholly the fault of the sod house that diseases were common. The common drinking cup, the open dug well, the outdoor toilet [or no toilet at all] shared the blame with the lack of ventilation and crowded quarters of the sod house

. . . . The floor was commonly of clay dirt. It was not possible to scrub or disinfect it of the millions of germs that found a breeding place in the dirt.

▲ Dr Cass G. Barns' opinion about the sod houses that he saw in Nebraska in 1878. He and his wife had just arrived to live on the Plains.

## Source D

. . . done my housework then made fried cake, pies, baked wheatbread and corn bread, cut out a nightdress and made it. . . . I am very tired.

▲ A diary entry for one day in the life of a woman in Kansas in 1873.

## Women had to make do

Everyday items like soap could not be bought. Women had to use what was available. There was no wood for fuel, so women collected dried buffalo or cow dung and used it instead of wood. This was heavy work and women had to be strong. Even when goods were available, like new pots and pans, families were often too poor to buy them.

Women made clothes for children and patchwork quilts out of old clothes. If they owned sheep they would spin and weave cloth. The women had to teach the children to read and write, as well as help to plough the fields.

## A lonely life

Perhaps the worst thing was the loneliness. The nearest neighbours could live miles away. Sometimes women were left alone for days when their husbands went hunting or to the nearest town for supplies. Loneliness, despair and the constant howling of the prairie winds drove some women mad.

## More settlers arrive

As more settlers arrived small communities grew up. This made life easier. People could now visit their neighbours.

There would be a general store where homesteaders could buy necessities, if they had the money. Schools and churches were built which gave people the chance to meet up. By the 1880s some community activities were being organized.

In 1885 something special was arranged in the town of Cheyenne. This town was at the end of the Kansas Pacific Railroad. The town was entertained by the Covent Garden Opera Company on tour from England! This does not mean, however, that all the problems of surviving on the Plains had been solved.

## 6.4 How did the homesteaders adapt to the Plains?

### Their first aim was to survive
If they had good soil and managed to cope with the weather, many homesteaders were able to succeed. When they arrived on the Plains their first aim was to grow enough food for the family to survive. Then, year by year, they ploughed up more land and grew enough crops to sell. The money raised meant they could buy better machinery.

### Learning to adapt
Successful homesteaders **adapted** to their surroundings. Those on the High Plains soon realized that they could not grow crops very well. They turned to keeping animals such as cattle and sheep. Some homesteaders in Kansas and Nebraska realized that their soil was more suited to growing wheat than corn (maize).

### Laughing at their troubles
One newly arrived homesteader commented to a neighbour:

> 'This would be a fine country if we just had water.'
> 'Yes,' said the neighbour, loading his wagon to leave, 'so would Hell.'

### Did all homesteaders succeed on the Plains?
Unfortunately, not all homesteaders could make a living from their farms. They could not cope with the problems you read about on page 66. Some homesteaders were hit hard by the droughts of the 1870s and 1880s. Many families faced starvation. The US army had to be brought in to give out food.

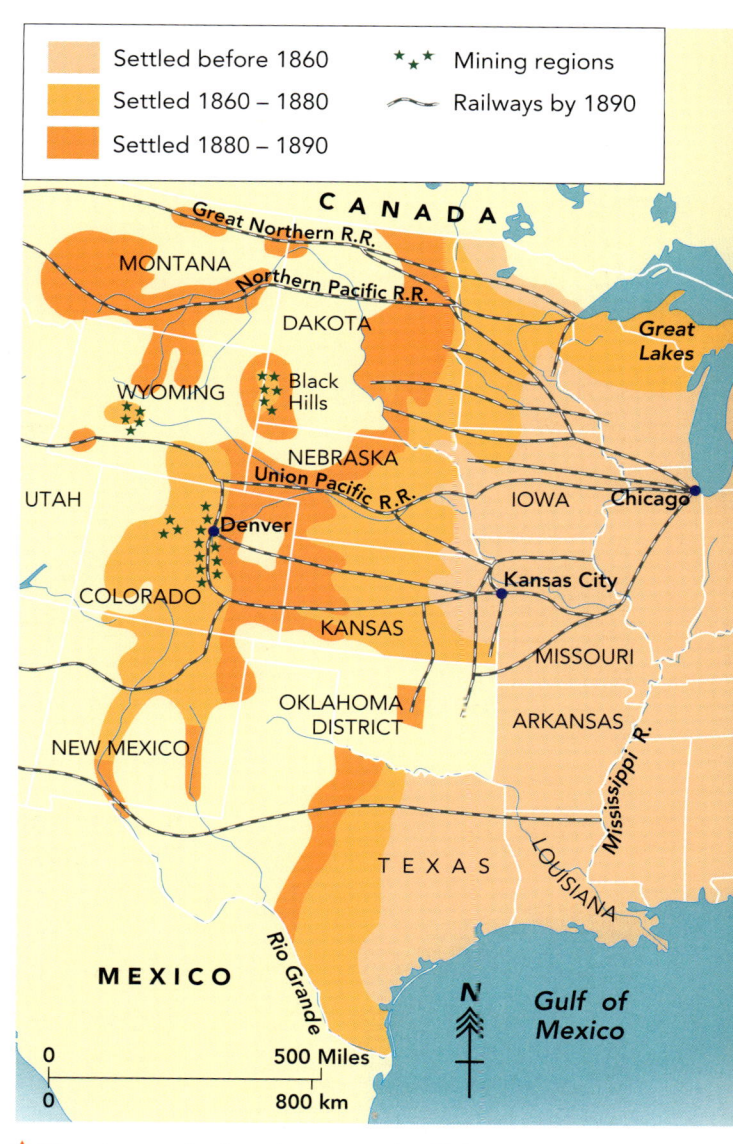

▲ The stages of migration on to the Plains.

## Inventions and techniques which helped the homesteaders

**New crops**
Some changes in crops have been mentioned. Also, Russian settlers brought Turkey Red Wheat with them. This grew well on the Plains.

**Better machinery**
John Deere invented a strong plough which cut into the hard Prairie soil and turned it over. It was called the sod-buster. Later more machines were invented – reapers, binders and threshing machines.

**Water**
A **windpump** was invented to pump water out of deep wells. After heavy rain or snow, farmers had to plough their land to conserve the moisture. This was called **dry farming**.

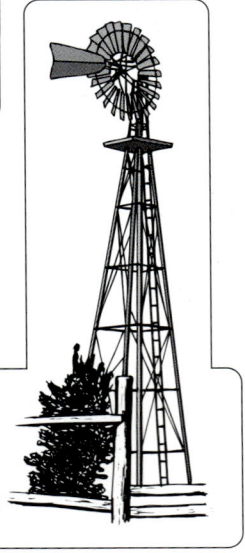

**Fencing the land**
Joseph Gliddon invented barbed wire in 1874. At last homesteaders could keep animals off their land.

▼ The Oklahoma Land Rush, 27 April 1889.

## Source A

70 CHAPTER 6 HOMESTEADERS ON THE PLAINS

## 6.5 What was the 'Sooner State'?

The US Government said that, at noon on 22 April 1889, it would open up another two million acres of farm land in Oklahoma. As the day got near people began to gather at the starting point. They were eager to get a share of the land. When the time and day arrived, a gun was fired. This was the signal that the 'rush' had begun. Between 50,000 and 100,000 people in wagons and on horseback raced to stake their claim to land.

Of course some cheated. They hid themselves on the land they wanted the night before! These people became known as 'sooners'. Oklahoma became known as the 'Sooner State'. In 1893 six million more acres were released. Almost 60 years before, this same land had been promised to the Cherokee Indians to keep forever. The West was changing fast.

### SUMMARY

- Many homesteaders had to live in dirty sod houses.
- In the 1880s homesteaders moved on to the High Plains area.
- Some homesteaders were successful because of new inventions like the sod buster, Turkey Red Wheat and dry farming.
- The Oklahoma Land Rush of 1889 made more land available.

## 6.6 The American Dream

Many of the early settlers and homesteaders were lured by the 'American Dream'. This was the idea that those who had 'true grit' and determination would be rewarded. You would succeed if you worked hard enough.

Success to most Americans at the time meant owning land. The settlers thought the West had plenty of this for them to take.

Paintings like Source 1 showed the American Dream come true. It was a far cry from real life in the West.

**Source 1**

▶ A painting called *The Western Farmers' Home*. It was painted for the benefit of Americans in the eastern states.

CHAPTER 7

# HOW WILD WAS THE WEST?

The Wild West: these three words seem to go together, thanks to all the Hollywood cowboy films. Perhaps the wildness has been exaggerated but keeping law and order certainly was difficult.

**Why was there disorder in the West?**
- The West was a huge area and it took time to organize a system which made people keep the law.
- In the early days travel was very slow. It took a long time for judges, marshals and sheriffs to actually reach some parts of the west.
- The mining camps and cow towns attracted criminals.
- Vigilantes (groups of ordinary people who tried to catch criminals and enforce laws) used violence and often caused terror.

▲ The states and territories of the United States of America by 1870, showing population centres.

## 7.1 Why was the West hard to police?

When the American Civil War ended in 1865, most of the lands to the West of the Mississippi River were still territories. Each territory was divided into counties and towns. They came under the control of the US Government in Washington. This was because the territories did not have enough people to raise the taxes needed to run services. There were also too few lawmen to cover such a large area. So when the Federal Government sent officials to govern the territories, lawmen were also sent – marshals, sheriffs and judges.

## Source A

▲ *The Vigilantes*, a painting by Rufus R. Zogbaum (1885).

## Source B

Five men were caught robbing a gambler and were given thirty-nine lashes each, but three were then accused of murder and an attempted armed robbery. Two hundred 'jurors' sentenced them to death. The trio could not plead in English, two being French and one Chilean. They called for an interpreter, but the mob was now infuriated . . . the wagon was drawn from under them, and they were launched into eternity.

▲ A description of a lynching in San Francisco in the 1850s. It was written by Edward Buffum, a journalist, who had gone West in search of gold.

## An example of lawmen in a territory

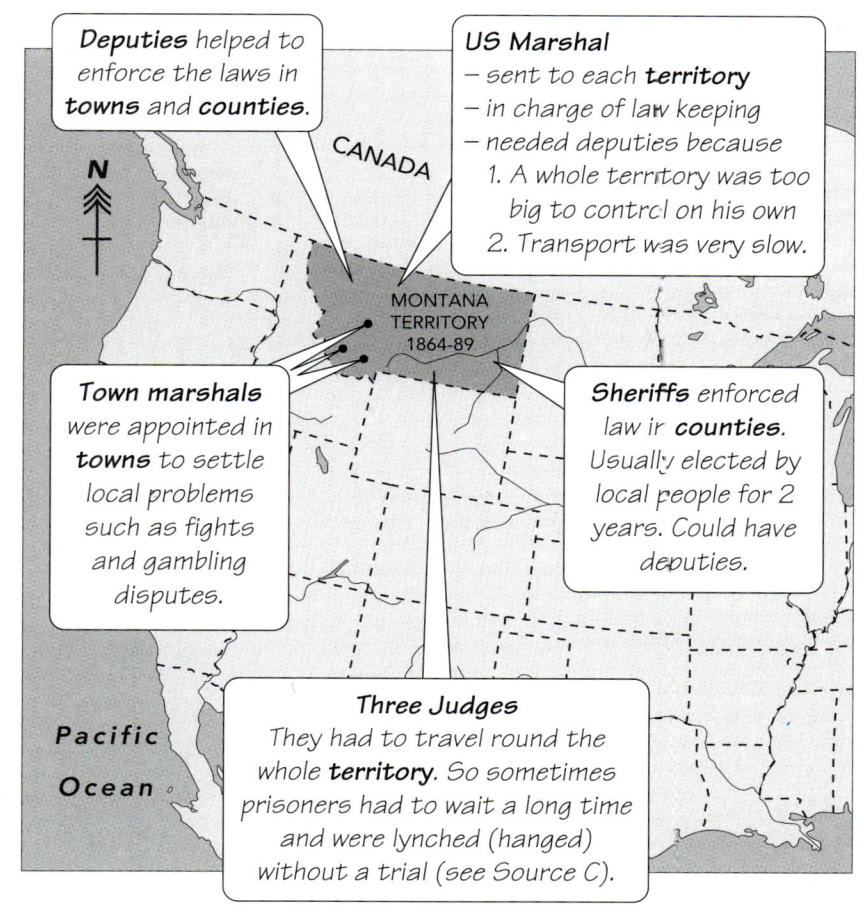

**Deputies** helped to enforce the laws in **towns** and **counties**.

**US Marshal**
- sent to each **territory**
- in charge of law keeping
- needed deputies because
  1. A whole territory was too big to control on his own
  2. Transport was very slow.

**Town marshals** were appointed in **towns** to settle local problems such as fights and gambling disputes.

**Sheriffs** enforced law in **counties**. Usually elected by local people for 2 years. Could have deputies.

**Three Judges**
They had to travel round the whole **territory**. So sometimes prisoners had to wait a long time and were lynched (hanged) without a trial (see Source C).

MONTANA TERRITORY 1864-89

CANADA

Pacific Ocean

7.1 WHY WAS THE WEST HARD TO POLICE?

## Legendary Lawmen

### Wyatt Earp

Wyatt Earp was born in 1848 and died in 1929. He started off as a buffalo hunter and a horse thief before becoming a lawman in the cow town of Wichita. He was sacked for fighting and moved on to Dodge City. There he worked as a deputy marshal between 1875 and 1879.

He is best remembered for the 'Gunfight at the O.K. Corral' in Tombstone, Arizona in 1881. There, according to legend, with his brothers Virgil and Morgan he overcame the 'bad guys', the Clantons and McLaurys. In fact, the evidence suggests that the three men who died were unarmed and shot in cold blood. In 1882, when his brother Morgan Earp was killed, Wyatt tracked down and killed the men that he suspected of murdering him.

### James Butler 'Wild Bill' Hickok

Born in 1837 Hickok is remembered as a scout and a fighter of Indians, as well as a gunman. Hickok is supposed to have killed a hundred men although only seven are documented. He served as marshal in Abilene in the year that the cowmen were banned from the town.

He was eventually sacked from his job in Abilene after accidentally shooting one of his own deputies. He once gave a young deputy a piece of advice, 'If you shoot a man, shoot him in the guts near the navel. You may not make a fatal shot, but he will get a shock that will paralyse his brain and arm so much that the fight is all over.' Hickok was shot in the back of the head by a hired killer in 1876.

### Bill Tilghman

Tilghman was poorly paid, but devoted to enforcing the law. He carried out his jobs in a professional way. Before becoming a lawman he had been a buffalo hunter and had a reputation as a crack shot. He was a very intelligent and crafty man who would chase criminals and use a disguise if necessary to trap them. He was not a 'trigger-happy' lawman but would use persuasion to get his man to surrender. He was a Marshal in Dodge City before becoming Deputy US Marshal in Oklahoma. He rounded up three of the most notorious gangs of robbers in the West – the Doolins, the Dalton Gang and the Starr Gang.

### Source C

The cow town marshals and their deputies deserve their fame. Their characters varied from good to questionable and downright bad, but the best of them replaced disorder and sometimes terror with the rule of law.

### ISAAC C. PARKER

Isaac C. Parker (1836–96) was one of the 'hanging judges' who brought law and order to the West by giving out severe punishments.

◀ From Robin May, *The Story of the Wild West*, 1978.

## The story of Henry Plummer
Henry Plummer seemed to be honest and law-abiding. But really he was a crook. He was elected sheriff of Bannack in Montana in 1864. Bannack was a gold-mining town.

Plummer was also the leader of a large band of robbers who called themselves 'The Innocents'. They robbed stage-coaches and committed other violent crimes while he was sheriff. He was eventually caught and hung by vigilantes.

## Other ways of enforcing the law
**The Texas Rangers** were set up by the Mexicans in 1820. Texas still belonged to Mexico at that time. Although only a small army of men, the Rangers kept order in Texas. They were feared but also respected.

**Vigilance Committees** were set up in some towns to keep law and order if there was no marshal. In some towns they were successful but sometimes they hanged the wrong person. In other towns they caused fear and terror. They settled their own private quarrels and sometimes hanged people purely because they did not like them.

## Disorder in mining camps
Gold was discovered in California in 1848 and in Montana and Nevada in the 1860s and 1870s. Gamblers, thieves, prostitutes and claim-jumpers were attracted there by the hope of gold. They made the miners' camps wild and lawless places.

## Who dealt with the disorder?
Even when the population became large enough to have a marshal, it took time for him to travel to the camps. So the miners tried to find their own way to deal with the lawlessness. They organized their own **miners' courts**. They could only settle difficulties among miners. Stealing, murder and violence by 'outsiders' were dealt with by the vigilante groups.

### Source D
To watch, pursue, and bring to justice the outlaws living in the city, through our courts

. . . No thief, burglar, incendiary [fire setter], or assassin, shall escape punishment, for any reason.

▲ The declaration of the first Committee of Vigilance of San Francisco in 1851.

### Source E
A general lawlessness prevails through Montana, Idaho, Colorado, Utah. At the bottom of this are these [vigilante] organizations. Everywhere they have brought trouble upon the community. The remedy is worse than the evils.

▲ A criticism of vigilante activity from the editor of the *Idaho World* in 1865.

## WILD ABILENE
Abilene attracted many people hoping to get their hands on a cowboy's pay. These included prostitutes, gamblers and saloon-keepers. In many ways, they were the cause of much of the trouble.

▶ Helena, a gold town in Montana, in the 1870s.

## Source F

## Source G

Newton is the fastest town I have ever seen.
Here you see young girls not over sixteen drinking whisky, smoking cigars, cursing, swearing . . . one of their townsmen says that . . . if I had any money then I would not be safe with it here.
It is a common saying that they have a man every morning for breakfast.

▲ A description of the cow town of Newton, at the end of the Santa Fe railway, by a writer in the *Wichita Tribune*, July 1871.

## Source H

His diet is Navy plug [tobacco] and whisky, and the occupation of his heart is gambling. . . . He generally wears a revolver on each side, which he will use with as little hesitation on a man as on a wild animal. Such a character is dangerous and desperate, and each one, generally, has killed his man. . . . They drink, swear, and fight; and life with them is a round of boisterous gaiety.

▲ An extract from the *Daily Commonwealth* a newspaper in Topeka, 1871, describing the cowboy.

### Trouble in Abilene
When the cowboys arrived at a cowtown like Abilene, they were in high spirits. They had been on the trail for weeks looking after the cattle and wanted to enjoy themselves. There was a lot of gambling and gunfights. Cow towns such as Abilene and Dodge City were wild places.

### A solution in Abilene
There was not much that could be done to make cow towns more peaceful until they had enough people living there to have their own officials.

In 1870 Abilene was able to elect a mayor. He appointed a town marshal to promote law and order. He chose **Tom Smith** who began to clean up Abilene. He was soon killed. Abilene's second marshal was 'Wild Bill' Hickok. While he was marshal in 1872, cowboys were banned from Abilene.

### Gunslingers and gangs
It was often difficult to tell the difference between 'good' guys and 'bad' guys. Plenty of people did rob and steal. Stories about them became exaggerated and they became heroes.

## Source I

▲ This picture of Billy the Kid is believed to be a true likeness (undated). Billy the Kid is very much part of the legendary West. His real name was either Henry McCarthy or William H Bonney. His career of crime began when he was 18 years old and in the Army when he shot and killed a blacksmith. He escaped from prison and became a hired gunman. He claimed to have killed 21 men by the time he was 21 years old! He was hunted down by legendary lawman Pat Garrett, who ambushed him on 14 July 1881. In reality, 'Billy the Kid' was probably responsible for the deaths of only four men.

## Source J

▲ John Wesley Hardin (1853–95). Hardin was a typical 'badman' from Texas. A hardened killer (see page 55) he boasted he had killed 44 men when the Rangers finally caught up with him in 1878. He only just escaped from Marshal Bill Hickok in Abilene after shooting a man for snoring.

## Source K

▶ The Wild Bunch. From left to right, Harry Longbaugh ('The Sundance Kid'), William Carver, Ben Kilpatrick, Harvey Logan and Robert Parker ('Butch Cassidy'). The Wild Bunch were a gang of cattle rustlers led by Robert Parker and Harry Longbaugh. Like other gangs of the time, they turned their hands to robbing banks and trains. Butch Cassidy and the Sundance Kid probably died in a shoot out in South America in 1909.

## Lawless ladies

Criminals were not only male. One of the most talked about women was **Belle Starr** (1848–89) who became known as the 'Bandit Queen'. She found gunslingers and gangsters very attractive. Belle took part in many robberies. She rustled cattle and horses and was the first woman in the West to be charged with the serious crime of stealing horses. She was sentenced to five years in prison. Belle Starr died after being shot in the back in 1889.

**Etta Place** was the partner of the 'Sundance Kid'. Together with Butch Cassidy they robbed banks and trains. **Annie McDougal** ('Cattle Annie') and **Jennie** ('Little Breeches') **Metcalf** took part in almost every sort of crime. They sold whisky to the Indians, they rustled horses and cattle, they robbed banks and trains. They were arrested and sent to a reform school.

## Trouble between cattleman and homesteaders

On the Plains the homesteaders and the cattlemen had reasons to argue.

- Homesteaders said that cattle wandered on to their land and destroyed their crops. This happened before barbed wire was invented.
- Cattlemen argued that their herds had to cross the homesteaders' land to get to water.
- There were arguments about who owned the land in the 1870s when cattlemen were trying to start ranches on the Plains.

**Source L**

▲ Belle Starr with one of her husbands, 'Blue Duck'. This photograph was taken late in her life.

### ANNIE OAKLEY

Annie Oakley (1860–1926) was handy with a gun, but she did not become an outlaw. She learned to shoot as a child. By the time she was fifteen she was winning shooting prizes.

In 1885 she joined Buffalo Bill's Wild West Show. This was a travelling show that gave people a 'taste' of life in the Wild West – cowboys, Indians, even an enactment of the Battle of Little Bighorn. Annie did shooting stunts. The musical 'Annie Get Your Gun' was based on her romance with Frank Butler, another prize-winning shot.

## Other problems for homesteaders and cattlemen

- Homesteaders and cattlemen who lived in lonely areas were in danger from 'claim-jumpers'. They arrived, killed and stole the land rights.
- When people rushed to claim land in Oklahoma in 1889 they were in a dangerous position until they could register their claims to the land.

These problems often caused trouble. The **Johnson County War** of 1892 shows how serious and violent the conflicts could become.

### Source M

▲ This is a photograph of farmers who staked a claim to land at Guthrie, Oklahoma in 1889. It was former Indian land and the population of Guthrie went from 0 to 10,000 on the day of the Oklahoma Land Rush.

# 7.2 The Johnson County War

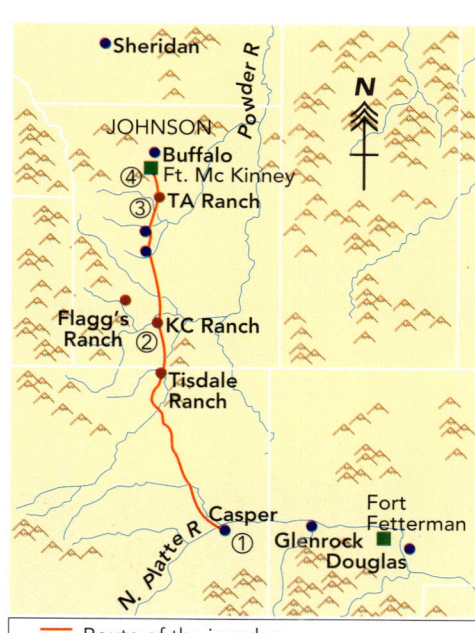

▲ Johnson County in the state of Wyoming in 1892.

Map key:
— Route of the invaders
① 'Invaders' arrived by railway
② Nate Champion and Nick Tate held out against invaders. Champion killed
③ 'Invaders' trapped by Sheriff 'Red Angus' and 300 supporters
④ US cavalry sent to free 'Invaders' at TA Ranch

## The Johnson County War

Johnson County was in the high plains of Wyoming. During the 1860s and 1870s, when farmers began to move on to the Plains this area was left empty. There were Indians in the area who tried to keep white settlers out.

## Which settlers got their first?

The first settlers were cattlemen who set up ranches. Some became wealthy. They formed the **Wyoming Stock Growers' Association**. When Wyoming became a state in 1890, the Governor joined this Association adding to its power.

## When did the homesteaders arrive?

The homesteaders moved onto the land in the late 1880s. When they claimed land the ranchers objected. There were constant arguments over land and water holes. The cattlemen accused the homesteaders of rustling their cattle. This was a hanging offence. The homesteaders said they had not rustled cattle. They had the support of Sheriff 'Red' Angus.

**Source A**

▲ An artist's impression of the lynching of Ella Watson and James Averill in Johnson County in 1889.

## How did the war begin?

In 1889 a rancher, called A. J. Bothwell, wanted to take over some land that belonged to **James Averill**, a storekeeper. Averill lived on the land with a prostitute called **Ella Watson**. James Averill accused Bothwell of being a land grabber. Bothwell accused Averill of stealing cattle. Ella Watson and James Averill were both lynched in front of their cabin. Neither Bothwell nor the lynchers were brought to trial.

## What happened in the war?

In 1892 Wyoming cattlemen decided to sort out the 'rustlers'. They hired some Texas gunmen. The Union Pacific Railroad even offered transport from Texas. This shows how powerful the cattlemen were. The plan was for these invaders from Texas to capture Buffalo, the county town, and kill Sheriff Angus, who supported the homesteaders.

The invaders attacked KC Ranch and headed for Buffalo. This attack warned the sheriff. He and local homesteaders forced the invaders back to TA ranch. The cattlemen used their influence to get the US cavalry to free the Texans.

There was little bloodshed in the war. Two homesteaders were killed (see map on page 79). The cattlemen were not arrested but they lost some of their power. The homesteaders continued to farm. The cattlemen fenced in their ranches. It was the end of the open range.

**Source B**

▲ An undated photograph of Ella Watson.

▶ An undated photograph of James Averill.

**Source C**

### NATE CHAMPION

Nathan ('Nate') Champion was a cattle rustler. He organized the resistance of the small ranchers in Johnson County. He held out against the 'invaders' at the KC ranch. After holding out for most of the day he was shot as he tried to escape from a burning cabin.

## 7.3 The end of the 'wild' West

By 1895 the problems of lawlessness were gradually being sorted out. There were several reasons for this:

- The expansion of the railways after 1869 made it easier for US marshals and judges to travel and enforce the law. The telegraph also helped people communicate faster.
- As families moved west they demanded law and order. Settlers moved for a better way of life, not to live in an area of violent crime. The banning of the cowboys from Abilene is an example of this.
- As more territories became states they made laws and enforced them. This improved matters.
- As state governments and town councils were set up, the shanty towns were replaced by properly planned towns. There were roads, piped water, better buildings and proper santitation. Improved surroundings led to better behaviour.

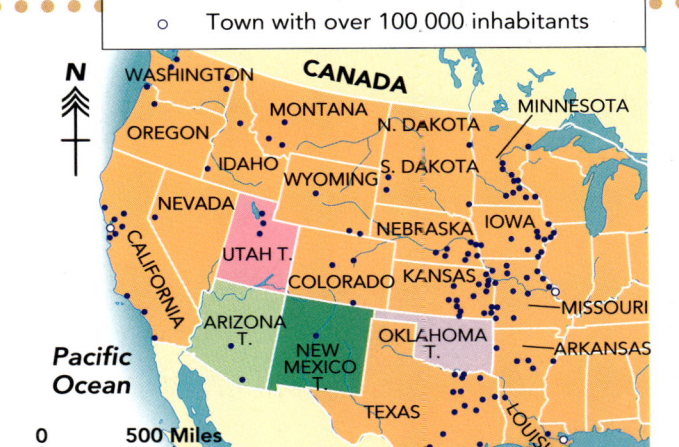

▲ The western states of the United States of America by 1890. Compare this map with the one on page 72.

But even in 1892 it was possible for law and order to break down, as it did in Wyoming, in the Johnson County War.

By 1895 the frontier was gone. There was hardly any area west of the Mississippi that did not contain white settlers. It was a victory for 'manifest destiny'. It was disaster for the Indians.

## 7.4 The Lincoln County War 1877-81

The Lincoln County War is another example of a 'Range War'. John Chisum (who had a huge ranch in Lincoln County, New Mexico) fell out with Major Murphy (a small ranch holder and shopkeeper in the town of Lincoln).

Alexander McSween (a lawyer) and John Tunstall (a rich Englishman) joined Chisum. They tried to drive Murphy out of business. Murphy decided to deal with McSween first.

He and his men surrounded McSween's house, set light to it and gunned down McSween and his men as they ran out of the burning building.

A cowboy who had worked for McSween wanted revenge. His name was William Bonney, alias Billy the Kid. He set out to kill Murphy and his men. Billy the Kid was killed by a Lincoln lawman, Pat Garrett. This ended the fighting.

# CHAPTER 8

# HOW THE PLAINS WERE WON AND LOST

'The last gunfire on the Great Plains between Indians and soldiers of the United States was exchanged on a bitterly cold day in 1890. . . On that day, on Wounded Knee Creek in South Dakota, a forlorn and hungry band of Sioux, including women and children, was forced and frightened into resisting Army authority. When it was over, the Indian wars of the Plains were ended and with them the long struggle of all the American Indians . . . to preserve some portion of their ancestral lands and tribal ways.'

**Ralph K. Andrist, *The Long Death*, 1964.**

The long struggle between the Plains Indians and the settlers began in the 1840s. The struggle ended with the Battle of Wounded Knee. This chapter is about that struggle, and why it ended in disaster for the Indians.

## 8.1 Why did the Indians go on the warpath?

Wherever white settlers went in the West they disrupted and almost destroyed the lifestyle of the Indians. Some Indians, like the Nez Perce in Oregon, accepted the white settler's lifestyle. The more warlike tribes resisted and defended their lands and way of life.

### The permanent Indian frontier
In 1834 the Great Plains had been given to all the Indian tribes as their land by the US Government. It would be Indian country for 'as long as the stars shall shine and the rivers flow'. The eastern edge of the Plains became a Permanent (lasting) Indian Frontier. The Great Plains was a huge area where the Indians could live as they wished.

### The frontier is not permanent after all!
When the first white settlers crossed the Indian frontier to follow the Oregon Trail, the Indians were not too worried. They had traded with white people for many years. They had drunk their whisky and caught their diseases like smallpox and measles.

### Source A

They are starving half the year. The travel upon the trail drives the buffalo off. . .

Their women are pinched with want and their children are constantly crying with hunger.

▲ Thomas Fitzpatrick, the Indian Agent for the US Government in the Upper Platte and Arkansas River country describing the Indian tribes. He was reporting to the Government in 1853, on the effect of the wagon trains on the Oregon Trail crossing Indian land.

### Source B

▲ A painting by Oscar Berninghaus (1874–1952) called *Indians Watching the Wagon Train*.

As more and more settlers crossed the Indian frontier to go to California to find gold (from 1848), the Indians felt they were being 'invaded'. The travellers shot the buffalo and brought another disease, cholera, to the Plains.

### The Indians attack
So the Indians attacked wagon trains and lonely homesteads. The settlers were horrified. They felt they had done nothing to anger the Indians.

### The army makes the situation worse
The Government sent units of the US army to protect travellers. Unfortunately, some army officers were not very good at dealing with the Indians. They certainly did not understand the Indian way of life. So tension and suspicion grew.

### A new treaty at Fort Laramie
By 1851 the US Government had decided that it wanted some of the Indian land for white settlers. The Indians were persuaded to move on to smaller areas of land. White settlers would not enter this land.

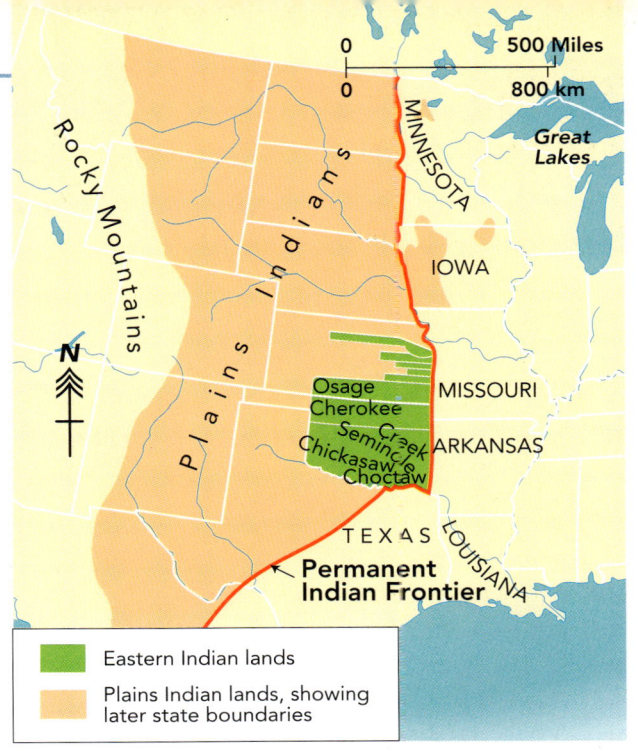

▲ This map shows the permanent Indian frontier and Indian lands on the Great Plains.

### Another broken treaty
But the Fort Laramie Treaty of 1851 was soon broken by the US Government. It felt it had been too generous to the Indians. In another treaty yet more land was taken away from the Indians.

### A new policy – reservations
By 1868 the government had a new policy. This was to put Indians on even smaller areas of land called **reservations**. There was not enough room for hunting. The Indian way of life was threatened. They would lose their self-respect. To survive they would have to fight.

## THE 'TRAIL OF TEARS'

In the late 1830s, white settlers wanted the lands of the tribes in the Mississippi Valley, so they forced the tribes onto the Plains. The Cherokees resisted, but were forced to go. Almost a quarter of them died on the journey West, so the Indians refer to the migration as the 'trail of tears'.

# 8.2 The Indians' struggle for freedom

There were four 'wars' between Indians and US soldiers between 1855 and 1868. These were:

- 1862 Little Crow's War (Sioux)
- 1863 The Cheyenne Uprising
- 1867 Red Cloud's War (Sioux)
- 1868 The 'Winter Campaign' against the Cheyenne.

## 1862 Little Crow's War

Little Crow was the Chief of the Santee Sioux. Little Crow and his people had agreed to move on to a reservation in Minnesota. Life was very hard. In 1861 the crops did not grow and about 12,000 Indians were starving. The US Government had promised to help but nothing happened.

Each reservation had an agency. White traders and settlers lived at the agency. They had been given the job of running the reservation by the Government. When some of the Santee Sioux went to ask for help they were sent away.

## Little Crow attacks the agency

Little Crow was very angry. He had tried to keep to the treaty but the white people had not done so. Little Crow felt that he had been made to look a coward.

In August 1862 the Santee Sioux attacked the agency buildings. Twenty men were killed and the women and children were captured. The Indians took food and provisions from the warehouses and burned the buildings. Later they ambushed a party of soldiers coming to deal with the trouble.

## Defeat for the Santee Sioux

There were more attacks on settlers before the Santee Sioux were rounded up by the Army. After a trial, 38 Indians were hanged and Little Crow was shot by a settler. The remaining Santee Sioux were sent to a smaller reservation in Missouri. The conditions were even worse and hundreds died during the first winter.

> **Treaties with the Indians**
>
> **Fort Laramie Treaty 1851**
> - made smaller homelands for the Indians.
> - promised the Indians that settlers would not enter these lands.
> - gave the Indians food, clothing, cattle and equipment for ten years as compensation for loss of land. This was reduced to five years, and in 1854 the Indian lands were reduced still further.
>
> **Fort Wise Treaty 1861**
> Sand Creek Reservation set up in Colorado for the Cheyenne. It was very poor quality land.
>
> **Medicine Creek Treaty 1867**
> The Cheyenne, Arapahoes, Commanches and Kiowas agreed to give up their land and move to small reservations in the south-east of the Plains.
>
> **Fort Laramie Treaty 1868**
> Set the territory of the Sioux nation. It included the Black Hills of Dakota.

## Source A

*If they are hungry, let them eat grass or their own dung.*

▲ The response of Andrew Myrick, a trader, on hearing that the Santee were starving. Myrick was murdered in the attack on the Agency. His mouth had been stuffed with grass.

**1876 Battle of the Little Bighorn** – Custer and the 7th Cavalry wiped out by Sitting Bull, Crazy Horse and the Sioux.

**1862 Little Crow's War** – revolt by Santee Sioux against bad conditions on reservations.

**1867 Red Cloud's War** – Sioux attacked travellers on Bozeman trail. Red Cloud forced withdrawal of army. Destroyed forts on the trail.

**1890 Wounded Knee** – final defeat of Sioux. Big Foot's band destroyed by army. Sioux forced to live on reservations.

All Indians located on reservations across America.

**1863–4 Cheyenne uprising** – Response to hardships on reservations. Starving Cheyenne attacked wagon trains for food. Army launched attack on Black Kettle's village at Sand Creek.

▲ The main clashes between the Indians and the US army between 1860 and 1890.

**1868 Winter Campaign** – Army campaign against the Cheyenne. Custer and Sheridan attacked Black Kettle's village on the Washita.

## Source B

We have waited a long time. We have no food, but here are stores filled with food. We ask you to help us get food, or we will keep ourselves from starving.

▲ A comment made by Little Crow, who had kept to the terms of the treaty of 1861.

## Source C

I ordered the men to begin killing them. . . . They lost . . . some twenty-six killed and thirty wounded. . . . I burnt up their lodges and everything I could.

▲ Major Jacob Downing who led the attack on the Cheyenne village in Cedar Canyon in 1864.

## Source D

You have no idea of the panic everywhere in this country. The most horrible massacres have been committed; children nailed alive to trees, women violated, all that horrible ingenuity could devise.

▲ General John Pope of the US army describing attacks on settlers by Little Crow's tribe.

8.2 THE INDIANS STRUGGLE FOR FREEDOM

## The Cheyenne's Uprising 1863
Black Kettle was chief of the Cheyenne. He was a peaceful man and agreed to the Fort Wise treaty of 1861. He moved his people on to the Sand Creek Reservation.

## Starvation for the Cheyenne
The land was very dry. Nothing would grow. In 1863 no buffalo could be found. The Cheyenne were starving. They attacked wagons and stole food, but no travellers were hurt.

## The army gets revenge
When the army heard about this they went on the attack. Black Kettle sent a peace party out, but the Indians in the peace party were shot. Their village was destroyed.

## Enter Colonel Chivington
Colonel Chivington had the job of protecting settlers and dealing with the Indians. His aim was to kill as many Indians as possible. Any Indian tribe wanting peace had to report to an army fort. The Cheyenne reported to Chivington. He chose not to understand that Black Kettle wanted peace.

## Massacre at Sand Creek
At dawn on 29 November 1864, Chivington's men attacked Black Kettle's camp. Black Kettle raised the American flag and the white flag of peace. He believed that the army would respect these flags and his people would be safe. At least 163 Cheyenne were butchered. This was called the **Sand Creek Massacre**. It was one of the cruellest acts in the history of the West.

### Source E
Black Kettle ran from his lodge shouting... Then cannon and rifle fire swept through the camp. Few of the Cheyenne had arms or any opportunity to obtain them because the first overwhelming charges drove them away from their lodges... Here and there, braves with weapons attempted to make stands in hollows or pits in the creek bank to protect women and children.

▲ Ralph K. Andrist, *The Long Death*, 1964.

### Source F
Some thirty or forty squaws, collected in a hole for protection... sent out a little girl about six years old with a white flag on a stick. She was shot and killed.... I saw quite a number of infants in arms killed by their mothers.

▲ From an eyewitness account by Robert Bent, a half-cast Cheyenne, who was in Black Kettle's camp that day. His sickening description of what he saw was supported by some of the soldiers' accounts of their own actions.

### Source G
It looked too hard for me to see children on their knees begging for their lives, having their brains beaten out like dogs.

▲ Captain Silas Soule who was present at the attack, but refused to order his men to fire on the Indians.

### Source H
At daylight this morning I attacked a Cheyenne village of ....about 900 to a 1,000 warriors. We killed... between four and five hundred. All died nobly.

▲ Chivington's report of his achievements immediately after the attack.

## Source I

▲ Chivington and his men attack Black Kettle's camp at Sand Creek. Painted by Robert Lindreux in 1936.

## Source J

All did what was expected of them. Colorado soldiers have again covered themselves with glory.

▲ From a report of the Sand Creek Massacre in the *Denver News*.

## Source K

I never saw more bravery displayed by any set of people on the face of the earth than by these Indians.

▲ Major Anthony, a US cavalryman, who was present at the massacre.

# COLONEL J. M. CHIVINGTON

John Chivington came from Ohio. He felt that the only way to stop fighting between the Indians and the whites was to kill all Indians. When officers objected that many of the Indians at Sand Creek were women and children he said this did not matter. They had to go and kill all of them anyway. 'Nits become lice,' he said. Of the 133 killed at Sand Creek, 105 were women and children.

At first the news of what happened at Sand Creek was reported as a great victory. Then it became more widely known what exactly had happened. To his surprise, Chivington saw he was not seen as a hero any more. There was even a chance that he would have to face a court-martial. To avoid this he resigned from the army. He went back to Ohio, where he became active in local politics.

## The results of the Sand Creek Massacre

Black Kettle managed to escape and continued to work for peace. The Sioux, Arapaho, Kiowa and Comanche Indians joined together with the Cheyenne and attacked white settlements. This became very violent because the Indians, as well as being skilful horsemen, now had guns. However, the army was able to move faster because of the railway. Hundreds of settlers were attacked or had to leave their homes for safety.

## Peace at Medicine Lodge Creek

In 1867 most of the Indians made peace at Medicine Lodge Creek. They agreed to live on the small reservations. They were tired of war and they accepted that their traditional way of life could not continue. Red Cloud, chief of the Oglala Sioux, refused to give in.

## The Bozeman Trail

Then gold was discovered in the Rocky Mountains in Montana. There was a rush of gold diggers and a new trail was opened from the Oregon Trail to the new gold fields. A gold miner, John Bozeman, made this trail so it was known as the **Bozeman Trail**.

Unfortunately this trail passed through the hunting grounds of the Sioux. **Red Cloud** had been promised in the Fort Laramie Treaty of 1851 that white settlers would not enter his lands. So travellers on the Bozeman Trail were regularly attacked.

## Red Cloud's War

In 1866, the US Government decided it had to take action. Talks began with Red Cloud but the army was ordered to build forts along the trail to protect travellers.

Red Cloud was furious. He withdrew from the talks and began to attack the workers building the forts and soldiers protecting them. He was joined by two other Sioux leaders, **Crazy Horse** and **Sitting Bull**.

In December 1866 a large group of soldiers led by Captain Fetterman left Fort Kearney to protect the woodcutters who were building the forts. They were ambushed by the Sioux and about 100 soldiers were killed.

In the spring of 1867 the Government agreed to abandon the forts. As the soldiers left, the forts were burnt to the ground by the Indians.

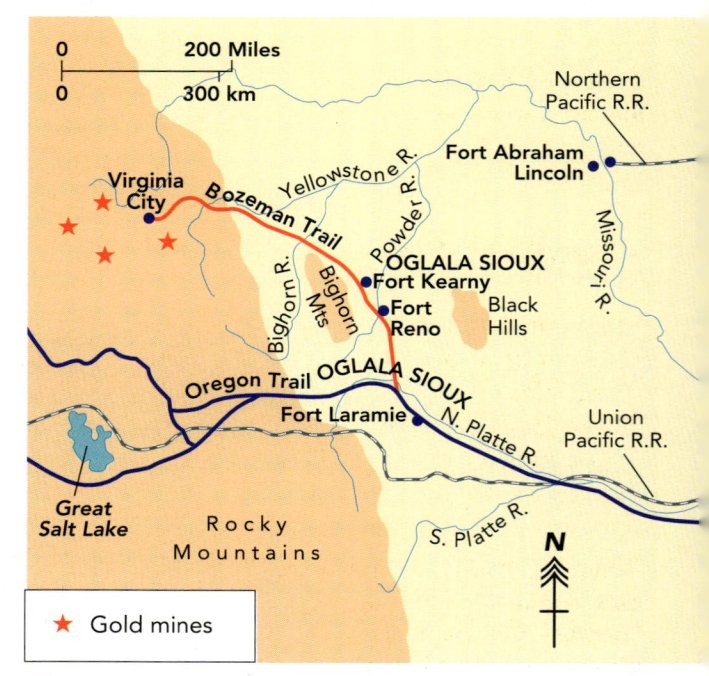

▲ The Bozeman Trail and the line of forts built by the army.

### Source L

◀ A painting by Schreyvogel of the Battle of Washita showing the attack at dawn by Custer's 7th cavalry.

### Source M

I do not understand how the massacre of Fetterman's party could have been so complete. . . . We must get our revenge on the Sioux, even exterminating, men, women and children.

▲ General William Tecumseh Sherman, who was in charge of military operations on the Plains, in 1868.

### Source N

If a white man commits murder and robs, we hang him or send him to the prison; if an Indian does the same, we give him more blankets.

▲ General Philip Sheridan at the outset of the 'Winter Campaign'. Sheridan, like Sherman and Chivington before him, saw no alternative to the Indian problem but to exterminate them.

## The Fort Laramie Treaty 1868

It seemed like a victory for Red Cloud but it was short lived. Red Cloud finally agreed to the Fort Laramie Treaty in 1868. This set up the Great Sioux Reservation which included the **Bighorn Mountains** and the **Black Hills of Dakota**. White settlers were not allowed to enter these lands. Young chieftans, such as Crazy Horse and Sitting Bull, did not agree with the treaty.

Some officers in the army decided that they would deal with the Indians once and for all. They realized that the Indians did not fight in the winter. So, in 1868, when the Cheyenne started to attack settlers again, the army decided to have a winter campaign.

## The Winter Campaign 1868

General **Sherman** brought in **George Armstrong Custer**. He had been court martialled and suspended from duty in 1867. With General **Sheridan** they planned a surprise dawn attack on Black Kettle's village on the Washita River. It became known as the **Battle of Washita**. Black Kettle's village was flying the white flag to show his people were peaceful. The sleeping Indians had no time to organize themselves.

Black Kettle, his wife and 103 Cheyenne were killed. The majority were women, children and the old.

The Cheyenne were then punished even more. The Medicine Creek Treaty said that they could leave their reservation to hunt buffalo, but now this right was taken away.

### RED CLOUD

Red Cloud (1822–1909) was the Chief of the Oglala Sioux. He fought to keep their lands, but finally accepted the Fort Laramie Treaty in 1868.

## 8.3 Conflicting attitudes to the Indian problem

The attitudes of white Americans towards the Indians changed over time. We need to look back over the events to see how and why they changed.

Before 1848 the US Government gave the Great Plains to the Indians. No one else wanted to live on the land.

After 1848 many white settlers crossed the Plains. The Indians felt threatened and attacked the settlers.

The US Government decided that the land on the Plains should be shared. The Fort Laramie Treaty was signed with Indians in 1851.

After 1860 more white settlers arrived. The US Government took more land from the Indians.

Some Indians fought back such as Little Crow, the Cheyenne and Red Cloud.

### Source A

They made us many promises . . . but they only kept one; they promised to take away our land and they took it.

▲ An elder of the Lakota Sioux.

### Source B

There was a shout as is never heard unless upon some battlefield, a shout loud enough to raise the roof of the Opera House, 'Exterminate them !'

▲ A report by Senator Doolittle of Wisconsin. He is describing the response of the audience to a speech he made in the Opera House, Denver, Colorado in 1865 about the treatment of the Indians.

What should be done now? There were two very different opinions

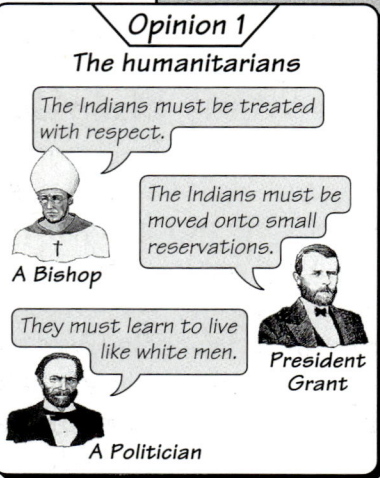

**Opinion 1 — The humanitarians**

- The Indians must be treated with respect. — *A Bishop*
- The Indians must be moved onto small reservations.
- They must learn to live like white men. — *President Grant*
- *A Politician*

**Opinion 2 — The exterminators**

- The more we can kill this year, the less will have to be killed next year. — *General Sherman*
- Complete extermination is our motto. — *Settler*
- The only good Indians I ever saw were dead. — *General Sheridan*

## Exterminators vs. Humanitarians

The '**exterminators**' were those white Americans who did not want to make any treaties with the Indians. They thought that the army should be allowed to wipe out the Indians. They were angry that the Indians had killed soldiers and settlers.

The '**humanitarians**' were those white Americans in the government who thought that the Indians should be moved on to reservations. They did not want to fight the Indians. They thought that this would only make the Indians fight back even harder. To try and make the Indians live like white people, the government had all the buffalo herds slaughtered. By 1890 there were hardly any buffalo left.

### Source C

▲ **General William Tecumseh Sherman.**

### TECUMSEH

Sherman was named after Tecumseh, an Indian chief who fought the British in 1812 and wanted a united Indian nation.

# 8.4 From the Little Bighorn to Wounded Knee

## Gold is found in the Black Hills of Dakota

In 1874 there were rumours that there was gold in the Black Hills of Dakota. This was the sacred land of the Sioux. It had been agreed in the Fort Laramie Treaty (1868) that white settlers were not allowed in the Black Hills.

## Trouble follows

By 1875 thousands of prospectors and miners were in the Black Hills looking for gold. The US Government tried to buy the land. Crazy Horse and Sitting Bull refused to sell. As Crazy Horse said, 'One does not sell the land on which the people walk.'

The Sioux were ordered back on to their reservation. They would not go. In the spring of 1876 the Sioux gathered in a huge village in the valley of the Little Bighorn. There were 1,000 tipis and 7,000 Indians. Of these, 2,000 were warriors.

## The plan

When the army located the Indians, an attack was planned. The plan was to advance from three different directions on the Indians (see map on page 92).

## The first problem

**General Crook** met Indians led by Crazy Horse. After a fierce battle he decided to go back.

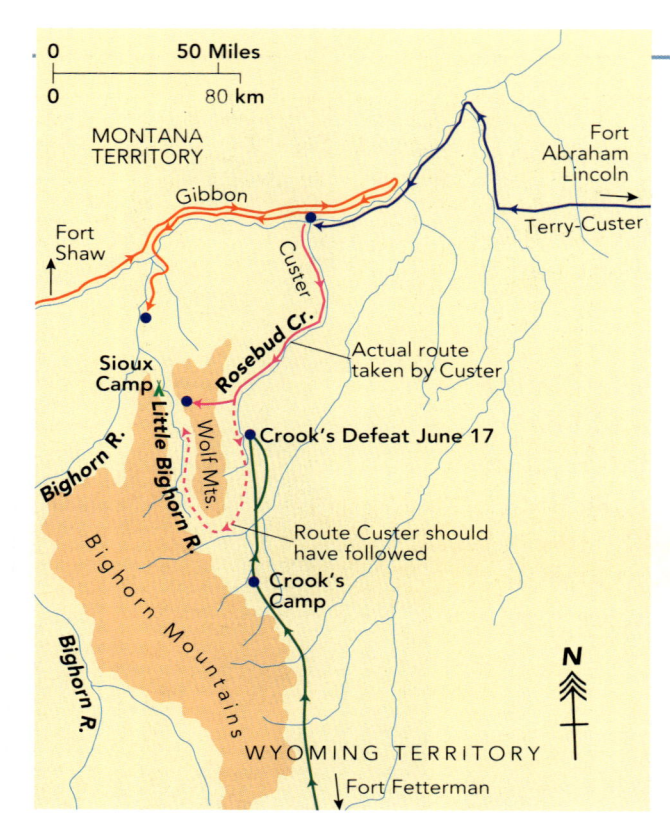

▲ The strategy of the Bighorn Campaign.

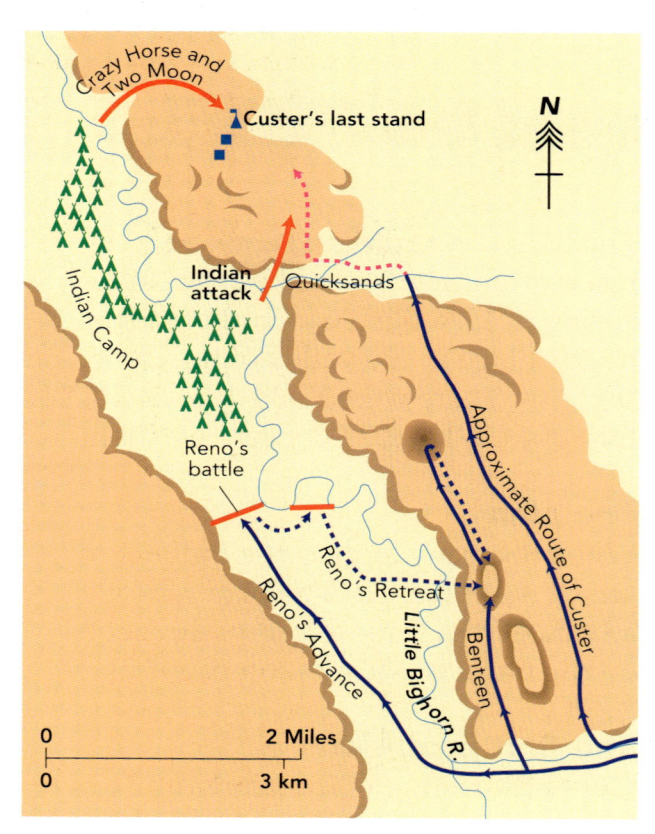

▲ The movements of Custer and his men at the Battle of the Little Bighorn.

General **Custer** was to travel along the Rosebud Creek and up the Bighorn valley. He was then to wait for **General Gibbon** and **General Terry** before attacking the Indians. The battle that followed became the most famous battle of the Indian Wars. It was called the **Battle of the Little Bighorn**. General Custer played a leading part in the battle.

## The Battle of Little Bighorn

Custer took 600 men and two officers called **Major Reno** and **Captain F.W. Benteen** with him. Custer's Indian scouts told him that the village had been seen. It was huge. They said that there was not enough ammunition to fight so many Indians.

## Custer ignores warnings and instructions

Custer ignored these warnings. He marched his men through the night and they were ready to attack the next morning. He was not going to wait for Gibbon and Terry. Custer, who had always been successful against the Indians before, was sure he would win again. Perhaps he wanted all the glory for himself. Perhaps Custer thought the Indians would run when they saw his soldiers. He could not have known that this time they were determined to stand and fight.

## More mistakes?

Custer divided his men, as he usually did, to surround the enemy. This time it did not work. Reno and Benteen were sent across the Bighorn River. They were soon attacked. Custer tried to cross the river but there were quicksands.

**92** CHAPTER 8 HOW THE PLAINS WERE WON AND LOST

### Source A

▲ An unusual painting of the Battle of the Little Bighorn by William Herbert Dunton (1915). It shows the battle from the position of the Indians. Custer is on top of the hill on the right.

He had to climb up the slopes above the river and was seen by the Sioux.

## Custer's last stand

Custer was attacked by Indians. They had Winchester rifles. He and all his men were killed. No soldiers lived to explain exactly what happened. The only eye witness accounts have come from the Indians.

## Did the Indians really win the battle?

The Indians beat Custer but their victory did not last long. News of Custer's defeat shocked all white Americans. The army decided to take revenge.

- All Indian reservations were put under army control.
- The Sioux were rounded up and forced on to reservations.
- Crazy Horse surrendered in 1877. He was murdered while in army care.
- All other Indians were forced on to reservations, even those who had not attacked anyone.
- The Indians had to obey the laws of the USA instead of their own tribal laws.
- Sitting Bull escaped to Canada.

### Source B

▲ One of the many photographs that Custer had taken of himself.

## Life on the reservations

Life was very hard for the Indians. There was not enough food. By 1890 there were almost no buffalo left. The Government had ordered that the buffalo be killed so that the Indians could not hunt them. Indians had to learn to live like white people. White people's education, religion and style of clothing were forced on to the Indians. Young braves became very frustrated. They had no opportunity to show their skill and courage. Then something very strange happened.

## The Ghost Dance

An Indian called **Wovoka** told the Indians about a vision he had. In the vision, white people were going to leave the Indians' land. The Indian dead would return to life. They would all recover their lands and live as they used to do. To make this happen the Indians had to perform the Ghost Dance. Unfortunately all that happened was that the Sioux became restless and excited. The agents and army became alarmed. This ended in tragedy on Pine Ridge reservation.

## The Battle at Wounded Knee

Pine Ridge reservation was at Wounded Knee Creek. What happened is not certain, but because they were worried about the Ghost Dance, soldiers tried to disarm a band of Sioux. The soldiers fired and killed 153 Sioux men, women and children.

It became known as the Battle of Wounded Knee. It was the last chapter in a very sad story. The army had its revenge. The white Americans had won the West. The Indians had lost everything.

### Source C

The inevitable explosion happened at Wounded Knee Creek . . . when warriors under Chief Big Foot provoked a battle with soldiers who were disarming them.

▲ H.S. Commager, *The West*, 1984.

### SITTING BULL'S DEATH

The 'Ghost Dance' incident made the government nervous. They saw Sitting Bull as the threat. He was shot on the Cheyenne River Reservation, in 1890, supposedly while resisting arrest.

### SUMMARY

- **1832** Permanent Indian Frontier established along the eastern edge of the Plains.
- **1840s** White settlers blazed the trails to the West; Indian tribes traded with Whites.
- **1848** The gold rush. Many more settlers. The Indians' hunting disrupted.
- **1849** Cholera came to the Plains.
- **1851** Fort Wise Treaty.
- **1860s** Homesteaders and cattlemen took over more and more land on the Plains.
- **1862** Little Crow's War (Sioux).
- **1863** Cheyenne uprising. Battle of Sand Creek.
- **1866** Massacre of Fetterman and his troops.
- **1867** The Medicine Creek Treaty, Red Cloud's War (Sioux). Battle of Washita.
- **1868** The 'Winter Campaign'.
- **1876** Battle of the Little Bighorn.
- **1890** Battle of Wounded Knee.

## The 'closing of the frontier' 1890
By 1890 the USA stretched from the Atlantic to the Pacific. There were white settlements all over the West. The frontier had disappeared.

## Manifest Destiny is fulfilled
There were now 44 States. There were only four territories left, which were soon to become States. The era of the pioneers was ending. The American people had fulfilled their 'manifest destiny'.

# 8.5 Evaluating General Custer

### Custer – hero or glory hunter?
Custer has been praised and blamed for the tragedy at the Little Bighorn. Was he a brave soldier or did he sacrifice his men for his own glory? Here are some sources to help you to form an opinion.

### Background information
- Custer graduated at West Point Military Academy. He was said to be too impulsive. He was last in his class.
- He was made a Brigadier-General in the Civil War for his bravery.
- He was devoted to his wife, Libby. In 1867 he deserted his post to go home. He executed 12 of his troop who deserted on the march home. He was court-martialled for this.

### Source 1
He was a flamboyant leader. He designed his own uniform which consisted of a wide-brimmed hat, trousers with a double stripe running down the seam, a sailor's wide-collared shirt, a red cravat, and on the sleeves of his jacket complicated loops of gold braid. Add to this the golden hair grown long and lying in ringlets on his shoulders and he becomes rather overpowering.

▲ R. K. Andrist, *The Long Death*, 1964.

### Source 2
A man of courage and energy who had kept the enthusiasm of a youth but never quite attained the judgement of a man.

▲ R. K. Andrist, *The Long Death*, 1964.

### Source 3
I have never met a more enterprising, gallant or dangerous enemy during those four years of terrible war.

▲ Major General T. L. Rosser of the Confederate army (army of the southern states during the Civil War).

### Source 4
A cold-blooded, untruthful, unprincipled man. He is disliked by all his officers.

▲ General Stanley. Custer served under him in a campaign against the Indians in 1872.

### Crazy Horse
Custer and Crazy Horse both loved to fight. Crazy Horse was skilful and daring in battle. He was devoted to his people, the Oglala Sioux, and also very religious. Crazy Horse was stabbed at Camp Robinson in 1877. He was buried secretly by the Oglala Sioux, who have kept the burial place a secret until the present day.

# INDEX

Abilene 51-2, 59, 63, 76
America 6-7
   American Civil War 13, 48, 50, 51, 95
   discovery of 4
   Great American Desert 6, 9, 14, 50
Appalachian Mountains 5, 6, 8
Averill, James 80

barbed wire 60, 61, 70, 78
Beef 50-4, 60
Billy the Kid 77
Black Elk 28
Black Kettle 84-8, 89
Bodmer Karl 28
Bozeman Trail 88
Bridger, Jim 29, 30, 41
Buffalo 16-19, 32, 49, 90-1, 93
Butch Cassidy 77, 78

California 6, 8, 14, 31-5, 42, 44-5, 75
Catlin, George 17, 21, 23, 24, 26, 28
Cattle barons 60, 79-80
Cattle towns 10, 51-2, 59
Cattlemen 10, 59-61, 63, 78, 79-80
Central Pacific Railway 47-8
Champion, Nate 80
Cheyenne uprising, 1863 84-6
Chicago 51, 52
China 47-8
Chisholm Trail 51-2
Chivington, Colonel 86-7
Columbus, Christopher 4
Cowboys 54-9, 61, 75
   the long drive 57-9, 75
Crazy Horse 88, 89, 91-3
Custer, George 89, 90, 91-5

Dakota 35, 62-3, 64, 89, 91
Desert Land Act, 1877 65
Dodge City 51, 52, 76

Earp, Wyatt 74
Ellsworth 51, 52

Federal territories 12, 72-3
Fetterman, Captain 88
Fort Laramie Treaty, 1851 84, 88
Fort Laramie Treaty, 1868 84, 89, 91
Fort Wise Treaty, 1861 84

Frémont, John Charles 30-1
Geronimo 22, 93
Gold 8, 32-5, 75, 88, 91
Goodnight, Charles 52-3, 58, 61
Goodnight-Loving Trail 52
Grant, President 90
Great Britain 5
Great Plains (see plains) 6, 9, 10-11, 14, 30, 50
Great Salt Lake 6, 9
Gunslingers 76

Hardin, John 55, 77
Hickok, 'Wild Bill' 74, 76-7
Homestead Act, 1841 64-5
Homestead Act, 1862 11, 65
Homesteaders 9, 62-71, 78, 80
   problems for farmers 66-7, 69

Iliff, John 53, 61
Immigration programme 63
Independence, Missouri 30-1, 39, 45
Indian frontier 10, 11, 81, 94
Indian Reservations 53, 60, 88, 91, 93
Indians 4-5 (see also Plains Indians)
   of California 34, 82

Johnson County War 79-80

Kansas 9, 51-2, 62, 64-5, 69, 88, 89
Kansas Pacific Railway 51-2

Lawmen 72, 74-6
Lincoln County War 81
Little Bighorn, battle of 91-3
Little Crow's War, 1862 84

Manifest destiny 11, 47, 64, 81, 94
Medicine Creek Treaty, 1867 84, 88, 90, 91
Mexico 42, 43
McCoy, Joseph 51, 52, 59, 61

Migration 11, 13, 29, 30, 32, 62, 69
Mississippi River 6-7, 8, 44, 63, 81, 82
Missouri River 44
Montana 73, 75, 76, 88
Mormons 8-9, 36-43
   Book of Mormon 36
   in Kirtland, Ohio 37
   in Nauvoo, Illinois 37-40
   in Missouri 37-9
   Danites 43
   State of Deseret 42

Nebraska 9, 62-3, 64, 69, 88, 89
Nevada 35, 75, 94
Newton 76

Oakley, Annie 78
Oklahoma 62, 71, 79
Oregon 6, 8, 14, 30-1, 93
Oregon Trail 29, 30-2, 40, 46, 82, 88

Pacific Railways Act, 1862 47
Parker, Isaac 74
Pioneers 8, 14
Plains 6-7, 9, 10-11, 14, 30, 40, 49, 53, 60, 78
   settlers on 62-71
   Indian wars 82-94
Plains Indians 14-28, 49
   Beliefs 23-25
   Chiefs 26
   Hunting 14, 15, 16-19
   Mandans 15, 17
   Marriage 22
   Medicine Men 24
   Sioux 14-15, 18, 25, 82, 84, 88, 91-94
   Soldier Societies 26
   Tipis 20
   Treaties with US Government 83-4
   Tribes 15, 24-27, 32, 37, 90-1, 93
   War with settlers 82-94
   War 27-8
Plummer, Henry 75
Polygamy
   Indian 22
   Mormon 38, 39, 42-3
Pony Express 45-6

Railways 10, 35, 42, 44-9, 51, 63, 64
Ranches 53, 54, 60, 78

Red Cloud 88, 91
Rocky Mountains 6, 30, 40
Salt Lake, the great 40, 41-3
Salt Lake City 41, 43, 45
Sand Creek massacre 86-8
Santa Fe railroad 64, 76
Santa Fe Trail 31, 32
Settlers 11, 13, 14
Sheridan, General Phillip 89, 90
Sherman, General William 89, 90, 91
Sierra Nevada 6, 8, 30, 47-8
Sitting Bull 5, 88, 89, 91-3
Slavery 13, 34
Smith, Joseph 36-40
Stagecoach travel 44-5, 49
Starr, Belle 78
Steamboats 44
Sundance Kid 77, 78
Tecumseh 91
Texas 10, 50-1, 53
Texas longhorns 50-1, 53, 78
Texas rangers 75
Tilghman, Bill 74
Timber Culture act, 1873 65

Union Pacific Railway 47, 67, 80
USA (see also America)
   Army 82-95
   Constitution of 12, 63
   Government 11, 12-13, 32, 42, 44, 47, 62, 64, 71, 82-3, 88
   republic of in 1783 5
   Territorial officials 73-6
Utah, state of 41-3
   Promontory Point 44, 48

Vigilantes 34, 73, 75, 79

Washita, Battle of 89
Watson, Ella 80
Wells Fargo 45
West, 'wild' 72-81
Willis, Ann 59
Wind pumps 60, 61, 70
Women
   Indian 19, 20
   life on the Plains 67-8
Wounded Knee, battle of 94
Wyoming 79

Young, Brigham 38-43